# RANDOM REMINISCENCES
## OF SIXTY YEARS OF LAW PRACTICE

### THE MEMOIR OF
## DEAN STOCKETT EDMONDS

# RANDOM REMINISCENCES
## OF SIXTY YEARS OF LAW PRACTICE

## THE MEMOIR OF
## DEAN STOCKETT EDMONDS

Rutledge Books, Inc.  Danbury, CT

Copyright © 2000 by Pennie & Edmonds LLP

ALL RIGHTS RESERVED
Rutledge Books, Inc.
107 Mill Plain Road, Danbury, CT 06811
1-800-278-8533

Manufactured in the United States of America

**Cataloging in Publication Data**
Pennie & Edmonds LLP
   Random Reminiscences of Sixty Years of Law Practice: The
      Memoir of Dean Stockett Edmonds
   Edited by Charles Miller

   ISBN: 1-58244-022-0

   1. Edmonds, Dean Stockett. 2. Lawyer. 3. Memoirs.

Library of Congress Card Number: 00-104399

The publication of this book
is dedicated to the hundreds of
"Pennie Edmonds" lawyers
throughout the world who over the years
have come to exemplify the principles and
teachings of their predecessors.

*As iron sharpens iron, so one man sharpens another.*

Proverbs 27:17

*... it was then, and ... is now, ... an institution in the sense that it was an established constituent of the business world of the day capable of carrying on as such indefinitely, the only requisite to that end being that younger men imbued with and devoted to the principles the firm has always observed, and of the requisite professional capacity, be brought along continually in readiness to and capable of carrying on in the same tradition when the older ones retired or passed on.*

— Dean S. Edmonds
1957

JOHN C. PENNIE
1883

PENNIE & GOLDSBOROUGH
1890

PENNIE, GOLDSBOROUGH & O'NEILL
1908

PENNIE, DAVIS & GOLDSBOROUGH
1911

PENNIE, DAVIS & MARVIN
1915

PENNIE, DAVIS, MARVIN & EDMONDS
1917

PENNIE, EDMONDS, MORTON & BARROWS
1946

PENNIE, EDMONDS, MORTON, BARROWS & TAYLOR
1951

PENNIE, EDMONDS, MORTON, TAYLOR & ADAMS
1963

PENNIE & EDMONDS
1973

PENNIE & EDMONDS LLP
1997

# UNITED STATES SUPREME COURT CASES OF DEAN S. EDMONDS

*Electric Boat Co. v. United States* (1924).

*Alexander Milburn Co. v. Davis-Bournonville Co.* (1926).

*Sperry Gyroscope Co. v. Arma Engineering Co.* (1926).

*Corona Cord Tire Co. v. Dovan Chemical Corp.* (1928).

*Sinclair Refining Co. v. Jenkins Petroleum Process Co.* (1933).

*Eastman Kodak Co. v. Gray* (1934).

*Chandler & Price Co. v. Brandtjen & Kluge, Inc.* (1935).

*Smith v. Hall* (1937).

*Maytag Co. v. Hurley Machine Co.* (1939).

*U.S. Industrial Chemicals v. Carbide & Carbon Chemicals Corp.* (1942).

*United Carbon Co. v. Binney & Smith* (1942).

# Partners of the Firm through 1999[1]

| | | | |
|---|---|---|---|
| John C. Pennie | 1883-1921 | J. Philip Anderegg | 1946-1975 |
| John A. Goldsborough | 1890-1915 | Hubert Turner | |
| William H. Davis | 1906-1945 | Mandeville | 1947-1960 |
| Charles J. O'Neill | 1908-1919 | Hubert G. Moore, Jr. | 1947-1980 |
| Arba B. Marvin | 1913-1933 | Stanton T. Lawrence, Jr. | 1951-1982 |
| Dean Stockett Edmonds | 1914-1972 | Clyde C. Metzger | 1951-1985 |
| Frank E. Barrows | 1915-1962 | Thomas F. Reddy, Jr. | 1951-1987 |
| W. Brown Morton | 1915-1968 | Frank F. Scheck | 1951-1991 |
| David Weild, Jr. | 1915-1970 | Robert McKay | 1954-1985 |
| Merton W. Sage | 1917-1958 | S. Leslie Misrock | 1955 - |
| Ernest H. Merchant | 1918-1951 | Charles J. Brown | 1956-1971 |
| Willis H. Taylor, Jr. | 1919-1982 | Robert J. Kadel | 1957-1971 |
| George E. Middleton | 1920-1955 | Keith E. Mullenger | 1958-1986 |
| R. Morton Adams | 1921-1930 | James G. Foley | 1959-1982 |
| Morris D. Jackson | 1921-1951 | Charles E. McKenney | 1959- |
| Raymond F. Adams | 1922-1949 | David J. Toomey | 1959-1977 |
| Leslie B. Young | 1922-1966 | David Weild, III | 1959- |
| Clarence M. Fisher | 1923-1963 | Harry C. Jones, III | 1961- |
| Louis D. Forward | 1926-1949 | Philip T. Shannon | 1964- |
| Daniel V. Mahoney | 1926-1966 | Sidney R. Bresnick | 1965-1983 |
| H. Stanley Mansfield | 1926-1953 | Barry D. Rein | 1965- |
| Donal F. McCarthy | 1927-1947 | Jonathan A. Marshall | 1966- |
| Hal E. Seagraves | 1929-1973 | Joseph J. C. Ranalli | 1968-1984 |
| Albert G. Davis | 1933-1937 | Berj. A. Terzian | 1968- |
| James W. Laist | 1933-1978 | Glen E. Books | 1969-1978 |
| Roger T. McLean | 1933-1949 | Gerald J. Flintoft | 1969-1999 |
| Harold A. Traver | 1933-1980 | George F. Long, III | 1969-1982 |
| Merton S. Neill | 1934-1974 | John L. Sigalos | 1969-1977 |
| W. B. Morton, Jr. | 1938-1964 | Joseph J. Catanzaro | 1970-1987 |

1. Time periods indicate total years with the firm.

| | | | |
|---|---|---|---|
| John E. Kidd | 1970-1986 | James N. Palik | 1987- |
| Walter G. Marple, Jr. | 1970-1987 | William G. Pecau | 1987- |
| Stanton T. Lawrence, III | 1971- | Catherine H. Stockell | 1987- |
| Charles E. Miller | 1971- | Mercer L. Stockell | 1987-1996 |
| Francis E. Morris | 1971- | James G. Markey | 1987- |
| John M. Richardson | 1973- | Thomas D. Kohler | 1987- |
| Samuel B. Smith, Jr. | 1973-1985 | Paul J. Zegger | 1987-1999 |
| Gidon D. Stern | 1973- | Jonathan E. Moskin | 1988- |
| Brian D. Coggio | 1974- | Jon R. Stark | 1988-1999 |
| William L. Grey | 1974-1981 | Darren W. Saunders | 1988- |
| John J. Lauter, Jr. | 1974- | Ilene B. Tannen | 1988- |
| Brian M. Poissant | 1974- | James W. Dabney | 1989- |
| Rory J. Radding | 1975- | Thomas G. Rowan | 1989- |
| Stephen J. Harbulak | 1978- | Scott D. Stimpson | 1989- |
| Robert M. Kunstadt | 1978-1997 | Ann L. Gisolfi | 1990- |
| Laura A. Coruzzi | 1981- | Scott B. Familant | 1990- |
| Joseph Diamante | 1981- | Todd A. Wagner | 1990- |
| Thomas E. Friebel | 1981- | Anthony M. Insogna | 1990- |
| Jennifer Gordon | 1981- | Brian M. Rothery | 1990- |
| Thomas A. Canova | 1982- | Brian D. Siff | 1990- |
| Geraldine F. Baldwin | 1983- | Arthur Wineburg | 1991-1996 |
| Allan A. Fanucci | 1983- | Isaac Jarkovsky | 1991-1997 |
| Victor N. Balancia | 1984- | Francis D. Cerrito | 1991- |
| Joseph V. Colaianni | 1984-1998 | Ronald M. Daignault | 1991- |
| John J. Normile | 1984- | Bruce J. Barker | 1992- |
| Peter D. Vogl | 1984- | Paul R. DeStefano | 1992- |
| Thomas J. Scott, Jr. | 1985-1990 | Marcia H. Sundeen | 1992- |
| Stephen I. Wallach | 1986- | Albert P. Halluin | 1994-1997 |
| Adriane M. Antler | 1986- | Kelly D. Talcott | 1994- |
| Samuel B. Abrams | 1987- | Alan Tenenbaum | 1994- |
| Edward R. Bannon | 1987- | William S. Galliani | 1998- |
| Donald J. Goodell | 1987- | Gary W. Williams | 1998- |

# Office Locations

**Washington, D.C. Area**

| | |
|---|---|
| 1883-1894 | 608 F. Street, N.W. |
| 1894-1924 | 912 G. Street, N.W. (McGill Building) |
| 1924-1931 | Washington Loan & Trade Building |
| 1931-1954 | 834 National Press Building |
| 1954-1971 | 13th and Pennsylvania Avenue (Pennsylvania Building) |
| 1971-1984 | 2001 Jefferson Davis Highway, Arlington |
| 1984-1993 | 1730 Pennsylvania Avenue, N.W. |
| 1993-1995 | 1701 Pennsylvania Avenue, N.W. |
| 1995- | 1667 K Street, N.W. |

**New York City**

| | |
|---|---|
| 1910-1911 | 5 Nassau Street |
| 1911-1920 | 35 Nassau Street |
| 1920-1942 | 165 Broadway (City Investing Building) |
| 1942-1964 | 247 Park Avenue |
| 1964-1984 | 330 Madison Avenue (Sperry Hutchinson Building) |
| 1984- | 1155 Avenue of the Americas |

**California**

| | |
|---|---|
| 1992 | 3000 Sand Hill Road, Menlo Park |
| 1992-1997 | 2730 Sand Hill Road, Menlo Park |
| 1997- | 3300 Hillview Avenue, Palo Alto |

# Table of Plates

i. Dean Stockett Edmonds, ca. 1940

ii. John C. Pennie, ca. 1914

iii. The youthful Mr. and Mrs. John C. and Alida York Pennie, ca. 1885.

iv. Dean Edmonds at the 1937 Christmas party in the firm's offices at 165 Broadway in New York City.

v. Frank E. Barrows, ca. 1950

vi. The legal staff of Pennie, Davis, Marvin & Edmonds on the occasion of the 1933 annual firm dinner at the University Club in New York City.

vii. The legal staff of Pennie, Edmonds, Morton, Barrows & Taylor at the firm's 1955 annual dinner at the University Club.

viii. The legal staff of Pennie, Edmonds, Morton, Taylor & Adams at the 1968 annual firm dinner at the University Club.

ix. Partners of Pennie & Edmonds at the firm's annual dinner, Pierre Hotel, New York City, 1996.

# Contents

PREFACE .................................................................. xix
FOREWORD ............................................................... xxi
INTRODUCTION ............................................................. 1
THE FIRM IN 1914 ......................................................... 7
MY ENTRANCE INTO
    THE PENNIE DAVIS ORGANIZATION ...................... 13
SOME EVENTS IN THE YEARS FOLLOWING 1914 ......... 20
THE BERLIN MILLS CASE ............................................. 25
WIRELESS TELEGRAPHY ............................................... 30
THE BESSEMERIZATION OF COPPER ............................. 38
MR. PENNIE WAS TAKEN FROM US ............................. 42
AIR REDUCTION COMPANY ......................................... 44
THE FULLER COMPANIES ............................................ 48
RADIUM LUMINOUS PAINT ......................................... 51
OXYACETYLENE WELDING AND
    AMERICAN METAL PRODUCTS COMPANY ............ 54
ENLARGING CLIENTELE .............................................. 58
DRY KILNS FOR TREATING LUMBER ........................... 67

RUBBER ACCELERATORS ..................................................................72

PELLETTED CARBON BLACK ............................................................80

UNITED STATES SUPREME COURT ..................................................86

RAINBOW LIGHT....................................................................................94

MACHLETT LABORATORIES, INC...................................................101

RETROSPECT........................................................................................108

EPILOGUE..............................................................................................114

ENDNOTES ...........................................................................................116

INDEX.....................................................................................................126

# Preface

In the summer of 1984 — I believe it was August to be more exact — when my firm was preparing to relocate its New York City offices from 330 Madison Avenue to its present location, there was a room in which a number of books and things had been stored in anticipation of moving them along with the rest of the firm's archives. As one of the users of that room, I had, from time to time during that sweltering summer, glanced at those old materials out of curiosity. On one of those occasions I noticed a typewritten manuscript sandwiched between numerous old and for the most part nondescript and forgotten documents. Thumbing through it I realized it was a memoir of Dean Edmonds, whom I had gotten to know by reputation prior to my joining the firm as an associate in 1971 and directly thereafter until his death the following year. Rather than relegate the manuscript to a continuation of its obscure existence, I kept it on a shelf "for future reference" in my new office at 1155 Avenue of the Americas, where it remained for a dozen years.

In 1996 for reasons (if any) I can't recall, I took the time to read the memoir in its entirety and, in a brief epiphany, realized its importance as an account — and perhaps the only account — of the firm's development over a significant period of its history. The memoir's existence was as much a surprise to the Edmonds family as it was to my partners who felt, as I did, that it should be published as an historical document from which the reading public would stand to benefit.

According to my elders at the firm, it appears that the memoir was actually one of several that were written in the late 1950s at the insistence of one of the then senior partners, Frank E. Barrows, who desired that the firm possess itself of biographical data about its members and staff. Mr. Edmonds' memoir is reprinted on the following pages exactly as he wrote it, except for the endnotes, some of which were contributed by me and some by the Edmonds family.

In acknowledging those involved in bringing the Edmonds memoir to publication, my thanks first and foremost go to the Lord for His guidance and direction, to my wife Fran for her patience and encouragement, and to Dean Edmonds, Jr., formerly Professor of Physics at M.I.T. and now retired and living in Naples, Florida, who graciously contributed the Foreword which includes useful and interesting insights into the history of the Edmonds family. Thanks are due also of course to my partners, for their encouragement, especially Leslie Misrock, who, as the most senior among us, has been successfully guiding the firm through the current extraordinary era in the development of intellectual property law; David Weild, whose own family history has its roots in the firm; Jon Marshall and Steve Harbulak who made helpful suggestions while serving with me on the firm's executive committee during the project; to Ed Henry, our executive director and keeper of ancient files; and to research assistants Kirsten Wegner, Kathy Iacovone, and

## Preface

Beatrice Su and last, but certainly not least, my secretary, Lisa Love, all of whom generously pitched in and worked patiently on the manuscript for this book. Any faults to be found in this work are entirely my own.

Charles E. Miller
1155 Avenue of the Americas
New York, NY 10036
June, 1998

# Foreword

My father, Dean S. Edmonds, was born on December 20, 1879, the son of a Civil War veteran and a small, dynamic woman, a veritable "little Napoleon," who presented her husband with no fewer than eleven children, of which Dean was the youngest. His father had been a cavalry officer who was seriously wounded at the battle of Gettysburg, and subsequently was given a soft job in Washington, that era's version of veterans' benefits. It was not a lucrative position, so that money was scarce and young Dean had to go to work at age eleven, serving ice-cream sodas in a Washington drugstore and struggling to acquire an education as time and funds permitted. He earned a law degree by attending Georgetown University at night but never did get into a proper undergraduate college or university.

Years later, when, as a wealthy New Yorker, my father sent me to the Buckley School, I came home one day to ask where he had gone to college. It seems that everyone at school had been talking about the great universities their fathers had attended and how they were going to follow in their footsteps. I (who was known to my childhood friends as Stockett) was of course asked where my father had gone and was ashamed to admit I didn't know. I well remember my father's answer: He looked at me very straight and direct (as he always did) from under his great, bushy eyebrows and said, "Son, I went to the College of Hard Knocks!" I was delighted to have this information and couldn't wait to tell my classmates where my father had gone to college, and to whence I would soon follow. It was some time before I found out why they laughed.

Hard knocks or no, my father had a number of things going for him. one was that he was a mathematical, or perhaps more precisely, an arithmetical genius. Although he never studied higher mathematics, he could multiply two four-digit numbers together in his head and come out with the answer just like that. He was, in fact, a walking calculator and, as such, gained entree to some of the highest levels of our national government and thus sat in the back of the room at many a meeting until some distinguished Secretary would turn to him to ask "What's the answer," to which he would respond immediately and with unfailing accuracy. This made him a popular character in various important circles, but it was only one of his many talents.

He had a dry but irrepressible sense of humor, and I well remember his big smile when something tickled him. On one occasion, for example, returning from a firm dinner in the years when he had become a senior partner at Pennie, Davis, Marvin & Edmonds, he showed me a special copy of the New York Times that had served as his place mat which the younger partners had arranged to read EDMONDS SUED FOR REPLEVIN BY FAN DANCER. After a good laugh, my father explained to me what replevin meant, and I never forgot his definition. Years later, when I sat in the office of my college roommate, Jeptha H. Wade of the Boston law firm of Choate, Hall, and Stewart, considering the return of property that had been improperly removed, Jeptha said, "We must have a writ of replevin," and I said, "of course." Jep looked at me quizzically and demanded to know how I knew what a writ of replevin was, whereupon I told him the above tale. I think he's still shaking his head over that one.

My father was an astute observer of all that went on around him, brought his incisive mind to bear on all he saw, and was known to "tell it like it is," his direct speech being nevertheless tempered with such diplomacy as the occasion might demand. His name started to become known around Washington, to the point where he could aspire to court a beautiful but very shy and retiring young girl whose station as the daughter of a successful Washington businessman was considered by many to be far above his own. Mary Watkins Arms was the daughter of John Taylor Arms, a prominent real estate operator and founder of the commercial real estate firm of Arms and Drury. He had built an elegant home for his wife and two children on Dupont Circle, and there Mary (who was to become known as "Mae" when she married my father and thus became Mary Arms Edmonds, although she was very embarrassed by and hated when people associated her name with that of Mae West) and her younger brother, John Taylor Arm, II (who became the dean of American etchers, with a series of etchings of the great French cathedrals that won him the Legion d'Honeur) grew up surrounded by books and art. I don't think my mother ever went to school, her father providing private tutors because he thought she would be bored in a school. Grandfather was right, as my mother-to-be soon knew most of Shakespeare by heart (her favorite toys being Bunny Orlando and Bunny Rosalind from As You Like It), could recite all of Dante's Inferno in the original Italian (one of the seven languages in which she became proficient), had mastered seventeenth-century European history, and, with a few close friends, organized the Attic Dramatic

Society, presenting Shakespeare and other classic dramas to a select audience in the attic of her Dupont Circle home.

It was natural that my father would be fascinated by this woman, who, behind her quiet, gentle nature, concealed the complete classical education that he had only barely been able to touch on and who, with her great knowledge of literature and the arts, was the ideal foil for his dynamic, outspoken ways. They were married in 1911 after a long courtship occasioned by my mother's feeling that her first duty was to take care of her father, who never really recovered from the premature death of his wife from appendicitis. I imagine rumors went around in Washington about the marriage of the poor but handsome rake to the shy and retiring heiress, but of course that interpretation was 50 percent wrong. My father was an investment genius, being an astute judge of management. He knew, almost instinctively, who to back, and thus, instead of running through the small fortune my mother brought him as the local gossips had predicted, he doubled it in a few years.

He also did well financially as a patent lawyer; he was fascinated with inventors and the advances they made in technology, and he became, in effect, a self-taught engineer, specializing in the law of patents. Although originally intended to protect individual inventors, the patent system became a sword wielded by big companies against their competitors. Thus, instead of meeting wild-eyed scientists with way-out ideas, my father's encounters were usually with sober citizens in charge of their respective companies' patent portfolios.

The present memoir abounds with stories of such encounters, of which I remember one most vividly. It must have been about 1929 when the two companies that controlled the neon-sign business in the United States — Claude Neon and Rainbow Light — decided there was only room for one of them and attempted to wipe each other out in one of the great patent litigations of the time. Given the irascible nature of the Frenchman Georges Claude, the vindictiveness of the people who ran Claude Neon, USA, and the machinations of the flamboyant C.V. Bob of Rainbow Light, a protracted trial was unavoidable. Even at my young age I was keenly aware of the situation, as the trial took place in Los Angeles, so that my father was away from home for an extended period and was eventually joined by my mother; my Aunt Mary, an older sister of my father's, came up from Washington to take care of the New York household and me. But the interesting part of all this is that in the course of the proceedings my father became very impressed with one of his expert witnesses — Raymond R. Machlett. My father's association with Ray Machlett, his original investment in Machlett Laboratories, his purchase of their first (and still operating) plant at the height of the Great Depression, the successful development of radar pulse tubes in World War II with the consequent addition of the power tube division, and the post-war world domination of the X-ray industry by the Machlett rotating-target tube exemplify my father's shrewd judgment in backing a little German glassblower, somehow knowing that this man would become the world leader in sealed-off power and X-ray-tube development and the head of a multimillion-dollar company.

Ray Machlett came to enjoy the good life, which included smoking the finest cigars he could get hold of, and also engaged in that day's standard method of testing X-ray tubes, which was to stand in front of them and see whether your ribs showed up well on the fluorescent screen behind you. Under these circumstances lung cancer was practically a foregone conclusion, and despite heroic efforts at radiation treatment using the latest equipment from the High Voltage Engineering Company, a new enterprise closely associated with Machlett, and the expertise of Professor John Trump of M.I.T., Raymond Machlett died in 1955. There was really no one to take his place, especially as a gentleman by the name of Hoffman, who had been groomed to take over if necessary, himself died shortly thereafter. Despite my father's talk about Machlett Laboratories' carrying on, he considered the situation sufficiently bleak to warrant his negotiating the sale of the company to Raytheon, under whose aegis it continues to this day as the country's leading producer of X-ray tubes. But my father never fully recovered from Ray Machlett's death. As his memoir states, the vacancy left by this man, whom my father met quite by chance in the course of a patent suit and who became one of his closest and dearest friends, could never be filled.

My father's memoir was located in the files of the present patent law firm of Pennie & Edmonds LLP by Partners Charles E. Miller and David Weild, III, to whom all who read these pages owe a debt of gratitude. Not only does it offer an insightful first-hand account of the practice of patent law over a significant portion of this century, but as I read it I felt as though my father were right there talking to me, and that if I looked up I would see him standing before me, cigar in one hand and the other outstretched in his characteristic attitude of dramatic exposition, telling again the tales I had heard so often so long ago. I am proud that the firm, after being known by a series of partners' surnames over the years, ultimately institutionalized its name by retaining only those of the founder and my father's. But perhaps my greatest source of pride is my good fortune in being the son of a remarkable man and the woman he adored.

Dean S. Edmonds, Jr.<br>
Naples, Florida<br>
May 1997

# Introduction

More than a quarter of a century ago, I began to think of my firm, Pennie, Davis, Marvin and Edmonds as it was then, and Pennie, Edmonds, Morton, Barrows and Taylor as it is now, as an institution in the sense that it was an established constituent of the business world of the day capable of carrying on as such indefinitely, the only requisite to that end being that younger men imbued with and devoted to the principles the firm has always observed, and of the requisite professional capacity, be brought along continually in readiness to and capable of carrying on in the same tradition when the older ones retired or passed on. After the lapse of many years I continue to think of it as such an institution.

"An institution is the lengthened shadow of one man," as is stated in one of our literary classics[1]; and if it is true of our institution, that one man is John C. Pennie. Davis and Marvin and I were more than twenty years younger than Mr. Pennie, and we, certainly I, absorbed much from him. Probably we absorbed a great deal without being conscious of it, and if we became conscious of it later, did not realize the source from which it came.

## Random Reminiscences

In time, perhaps after a long time, I at least became conscious of it. I realized that for about eight years I was in close association with a great personality, a man of high ideals who lived up to his ideals, a scholar with scholastic attainments extending over a broad range, a raconteur with a rare sense of humor, and a genial companion, held in high esteem by all who knew him and remembered with respect and high regard by all who met him.

Along with a brief outline of how it came about that I teamed up with Mr. Pennie, I am proposing to put down on paper a number of items connected with the firm. But it will not be in any sense a history of the firm for it will be mostly about myself and incidents in the firm's history with which I was connected.

So as this is going to be a personal record, I may well begin with something about myself.

I was born in Washington, D.C. on December 20, 1879, and I was educated in the public schools and graduated from Central High School in June of 1897. There was then a regiment of cadets in the High Schools of Washington, and, in my last year, I was a lieutenant in one of the companies, and on March 4, 1897, I marched up Pennsylvania Avenue in the big parade celebrating the inauguration of President McKinley, saluting him with my sword as I passed him at the reviewing stand. I told my mother that evening that the President seemed to look straight at me with an expression indicating strong approval and that as he looked at me, I thought I heard him say "Nice going," or something to that effect.

In the spring of 1897, there was a great exodus from and even a greater influx into Washington incident to the change of administration, the Democrats under Cleveland constituting the exodus, and the Republicans under McKinley constituting the influx. In those days, such a local upheaval was the usual

## Introduction

concomitant of a change of administration because "Civil Service" protection had not then made such headway.

The new regime in the Treasury Department came from Chicago, Illinois, and, through my oldest brother, Howard,[2] who lived in Chicago and had made considerable progress in the business world there, I was offered a minor clerkship in the Treasury Department at what seemed a fabulous salary, namely, $55 each and every month, and that was a fabulous salary then for an eighteen-year-old High School graduate. Perhaps I should have gone to college then and perhaps the fabulous salary prevailed. Anyway, I took the job and I was assigned to the Bureau of Navigation, and in the fall I entered the law school of Georgetown University where the sessions started at 6:30 in the evening.

I had one very interesting experience as an employee of that Bureau of Navigation, an experience which developed considerably my knowledge of advocacy and the processes of legislation. There was a proposal on then for subsidizing the American Merchant Marine and much of the work in connection with the proposed legislation devolved upon the Commissioner of Navigation. I was able to give him the help he needed in preparing an elaborate series of tables showing what amounts of subsidy would be payable, graduated upon the tonnage, speed and number of trips per year of a merchant vessel. Preparing these tables was not very difficult, but the task got assigned to the Commissioner's feminine secretary and me because the level of intelligence of the other employees of the Bureau was rather low; and when it came to an evening meeting of representatives of the big shipping interests and their eminent counsel, a meeting at the Arlington Hotel which was then the real center of Washington, the Commissioner's secretary could not be taken to the meeting because that was not done in those days and I was taken there as the only alternative. At the meeting, the Commissioner talked at some length about the proposed legislation, but soon the inevitable happened. Somebody wanted to know about the amount of subsidy payable under conditions he prescribed. The Commissioner could not answer the question, but I, sitting beside him, soon had the answer by reference to my tables. From then on, I found myself drawn into the discussions with all of these eminent gentlemen whenever the discussion got around to figures. Following that, there were frequent hearings before the Committees on Commerce of the Senate and the House, and the Commissioner always took me with him, and on a number of occasions I was forced to enter into the discussions to some little extent. Even the trip from the Treasury to the Capitol was a memorable one for me; I walked through the corridors of the Treasury Department beside the Commissioner, and we would go out on Fifteenth Street and summon a horse-drawn cab which would convey us along Pennsylvania Avenue and up Capitol Hill.

After some two or three years in that Bureau of Navigation, I got myself transferred to the office of the Auditor for the War Department as a step incident to securing an enlarged stipend, the new stipend being $100 per month, followed later by an increase up to $150 per month. That Auditor's office was in a building known as the Winder Building located at 17th and F Streets, across 17th Street from the War Department. My office was in the last room back along the F Street side on the second floor, and my father told me that that was the room in which he had officiated back in 1864 and 1865. My father was an officer in the Third Pennsylvania Cavalry in the Civil War and was wounded severely on the third day at Gettysburg. It took him months to recover and, along in 1864, when he went back to

## Introduction

Washington to report for duty with his regiment, an examining medical board ruled that he was not fit to go back to the front but could serve in Washington and he was made Judge Advocate General of a Military Court. This Court sat in that room where I worked forty years later, and the next room to it was my father's office as prosecuting attorney of the Court.

At the law school I received a Bachelor's degree at the end of two years, and continued through a third year when I received a Master's degree. Then I was told that there would be an examination for admission to the Bar of the District of Columbia in the following October and I took the examination and passed it and was admitted to the Bar. I have always thought that the Examiners admitted me because of my answer to the first section of the first question. With that answer I "knocked them for a loop" and they went no further. The first question called for a series of definitions and the first one of these definitions was given in my copy of Blackstone in Latin followed by a translation into English. When I came to this in my reading of Blackstone, I was much pleased to find that I understood all of this definition in Latin and could even translate it, with the result that the Latin definition stuck in my mind. I could not forego using that in the examination, so I answered the question with an acceptable definition in English and followed that with "or, as Blackstone says," and then proceeded with the whole of the definition in Latin. That, I am sure, got me into the Bar, where otherwise I might have failed.

Along in the late summer of 1902 I resigned from my job in the Treasury Department and went up to Schenectady in the Patent Department of the General Electric Company. A.G. Davis, the head of the Patent Department, made this available to me at the request of my brother, S.O. Edmonds, who was practicing patent law in New York City. In my new office I had the title of "Assistant Patent Attorney"; I may have entertained some doubt on that score but for the fact that some new letter paper was printed for the Patent Department soon after I arrived there and I found my name added at the bottom of the list and right under it was printed "Assistant Patent Attorney". That made it official. I may add that my compensation was not of the same magnitude as my title. The compensation was $15 per week. However, at that time, I did not know very much about either patents or electricity, so it may be that the compensation was all that was appropriate. Before long, I was able to hold up my end as an Assistant Patent Attorney and I stayed there with G.E. until October, 1905.

# The Firm in 1914

At the start of 1914, the firm as it then existed, under the name of Pennie, Davis & Goldsborough, had its office in the building known as 35 Nassau Street, extending around the southwest corner of Nassau and Liberty Streets. The firm's office was on the thirteenth floor of the wing of the building extending westward along Liberty Street as shown on the accompanying floor plan.[3] It was substantially rectangular with a large rectangular space extending down the middle, three rooms on one side of this open space with windows on Liberty Street, and three rooms extending down the other side with windows opening on a court. The room on the Liberty Street side distant from the entrance was Mr. Pennie's room. The room nearest the entrance on the Liberty Street side was Mr. Davis's room. Between these two was a much smaller room occupied by Mr. Marvin.

On the other side of the central space, the room distant from the entrance was occupied by Leon Rosenthal who was engaged almost entirely on foreign patent matters and soliciting U.S. patents for Bosch Magneto Company of Germany.

On this inner side of the office, the room adjacent to the entrance was where the accounting of the firm was centered and that work was under the charge of Mr. Davis' mother-in-law, Mrs. Collyer. She had one assistant, a little girl about three feet high who moved rapidly around the office without making a sound, and, because of that, was known as "the Mouse". Among other things, she answered telephone calls which came in at a small switchboard on a table just inside the office entrance door. In between the two rooms on the south side, there was a rather large room which was occupied at that time and had been for some years prior to that by one Clarence Hopkins, a talented but eccentric individual who did patent work at times but not with great enthusiasm for he was much more concerned with developing ideas of his own, primarily in the field of sound reproduction. Davis and I had known Clarence Hopkins in Washington when Davis was a beginner in the field of patents and I was finishing up at law school. We three would meet at times when Davis and I would absorb elementary instruction in the patent field from Clarence Hopkins with no realization of how relations would be reversed in the years ahead.

At the end of the open space of the office distant from the entrance were four desks for four stenographers.

This was the office into which I went at some time about the first of March, 1914, not, however, as a participant in the firm's work. Clarence Hopkins was offered and accepted a proposal of the Eastman Kodak Company that he take up residence in Rochester, New York, and develop his ideas about sound reproduction in association with Eastman. His departure vacated that room, the middle one of the three on the court side, and I was invited to occupy that room where I could conduct my own law practice, such as it was then. The circumstances out of

## The Firm in 1914

which that invitation evolved were unusual and I will recount them, but first a word about the men who were busily engaged in the practice of law in that office back there in 1914.

Mr. Pennie was born in Albany in 1858 and grew up there. His college education was at Union College, Schenectady, where he graduated in 1877. Following that, he went to Germany and studied there for a couple of years, principally at the Universities of Goettingen and Breslau, where he perfected his knowledge of the German language and literature and also, I think, became fluent in French. Following that, he returned to this country and in 1879 he was admitted to the Bar of the State of New York. Then in January, 1881, he became an Examiner in the Patent Office at Washington and worked there for about three years. Toward the latter part of his employment in the Patent Office I think he was in the Interference Division. Then he resigned from the Patent Office and entered upon the practice of patent law in Washington with his friend John A. Goldsborough under the name Pennie & Goldsborough.[4]

The business of the partnership prospered and after some years Mr. Pennie found that his professional work required that he make frequent trips to New York and spend much of his time there. This New York work increased to such extent that he finally decided he should have a New York office and he joined forces with three friends with whom he grew up in Albany in an office in the old Hanover Bank Building at the corner of Pine and Nassau Streets. These four men practiced under the name Herrick, Farren, Chase and Pennie, but I think it was not a firm in the usual sense, or at least that Mr. Pennie conducted his patent practice independently of the others.

At about this time, or a little later, Mr. Pennie found he needed an assistant and Davis, who had been working for some years for the firm of Betts, Sheffield & Betts and had become somewhat dissatisfied there, left that firm and joined up with Mr. Pennie. During all this period, Mr. Pennie kept up his Washington association under the name Pennie & Goldsborough, the Washington office being run by Charles J. O'Neill during the absences of Mr. Pennie. About 1908, Mr. Pennie reorganized his professional affairs by forming a Washington firm under the name Pennie, Goldsborough & O'Neill[5], and a New York firm under the name Pennie, Davis & Goldsborough.[6]

At about the time when this was done, his New York practice required more space than was available in the office in the Hanover Bank Building and the New York firm of Pennie, Davis & Goldsborough moved to the office in 35 Nassau Street.

At an early period of his practice, Mr. Pennie became engaged on some work in the field of metallurgy for which he was well qualified, and this led in the course of time to professional work for the New Jersey Zinc Company, or a company which later became the New Jersey Zinc Company. I think that work required that he make one or more trips abroad and evidently he handled the matters committed to his care with such expertness that the officials of the Zinc Company soon came to a full appreciation of his capacities, with the result that they sought his advice continually. It is interesting and a source of much satisfaction that the professional patent work for New Jersey Zinc Company started by Mr. Pennie way back there before the turn of the century has continued with the firm through all the years since.

Mr. Davis was born down in Maine where his father was one of the managers of the Katadin Iron Works. When the iron ore in that region petered out, the family moved to Knoxville, Tennessee.

Davis had an older brother, Albert G. Davis, who in some

## The Firm in 1914

way became interested in patents and took up residence in Washington for a time, I think, as an Examiner in the Patent Office. Evidently he made rapid progress in patent work and in some way his outstanding ability came to the attention of Mr. Frederick P. Fish of the Boston firm of Fish, Richardson, Herrick & Storrow, patent counsel for many large industrial companies including the General Electric Company.

Along about 1901, the then patent attorney for the General Electric Company in Schenectady died. A robber entered his house one night, and some noise that he made wakened the attorney who went after the robber, and chased him out of the house and down the street, whereupon the robber turned on him and shot him. Mr. Fish had to select a successor and he had been so impressed with the ability of this young Albert G. Davis that he put him in charge of the Patent Department of the General Electric Company at Schenectady.

Will Davis went to Washington and took up patent work, doubtless led to that by the progress his brother had made. After some years in Washington, he came over to New York as a young lawyer in the office of Betts, Sheffield & Betts, then one of the outstanding law firms specializing in patent matters. During much of the time while he was employed in that office, he participated in the work of the firm in connection with the Marconi patents. Later, as I have stated, he left that firm and went with Mr. Pennie.

As I mentioned, I knew Davis in Washington in the years around 1900 while I was attending Georgetown Law School, and I recall that along in 1903 or 1904 when I was living in Schenectady, Davis came up there in connection with a patent litigation in which he represented an interest opposed to the General Electric Company. I was much impressed because he was engaged in taking testimony in a litigation and so had arrived at a stage of progress in professional work well beyond the point I had reached.

Arba B. Marvin grew up out in the middle west and attended the University of Wisconsin at Madison, Wisconsin. Then for a time he was employed in the Patent Office and from there he went to the Patent Department of the General Electric Company at Schenectady and became one of my associates there. I did not see much of him there because he arrived only a few months before I departed about October 1, 1905. After some years with G.E. in Schenectady, Marvin went out to Chicago in the office of Parkinson & Lane, a patent law firm of some prominence in Chicago. Marvin was not very happy in that association which is not surprising because Parkinson died and Lane was a difficult person for anyone to get along with. Marvin was related to Davis by marriage and that, together with his dissatisfaction in Chicago, led Davis to propose that he come to New York with the Pennie firm, a proposal which Marvin was quick to accept. I think professional patent work never had much of an appeal for Arba Marvin; probably dealings in real estate had much more appeal, and I am sure he found a better outlet for his talents in the field of real estate.

# My Entrance into the Pennie Davis Organization

When I left Schenectady in 1905 and came down to New York, it was to take employment with an older brother, Samuel O. Edmonds, in an office in the Mutual Life Building at Nassau and Liberty Streets, a building which has recently been torn down to make way for a new building for the Chase Manhattan National Bank. After some years my brother and I began practicing under the name Edmonds & Edmonds, but it was not a firm in any real sense. In time it became apparent to me that I wanted to make a change in my professional setup and I finally decided to embark upon the practice of law on my own. That decision, as I recall, was a product of much hopefulness and a bit of bravado because my so-called clientele at that time was neither numerous nor important. Anyway the decision was made and I began to look around for an office, more particularly an office which would be adequately impressive and also would be obtainable at a very modest rent. Somehow my ideas got centered upon an office in the Liberty Tower Building on the northwest corner of Nassau and Liberty Streets, an office up on the twelfth floor facing on Liberty Street. One day I was walking up Liberty Street toward Broadway thinking of whether or not I wanted to cast my lot there in that Liberty Tower Building and I stopped at the curb near the entrance to 35 Nassau Street and stood there looking up at my prospective office across the street. While standing there, someone bumped into me inadvertently and the two of us looked each at the other at the same time and I found that the man who had walked into me and nearly pushed me off the curb was Will Davis. He recognized me at the same time and said, "Why do you stand here looking up at the high buildings?" I told him briefly that I was thinking of embarking upon the practice of law on my own and was considering whether I wanted to take an office up in that Liberty Tower Building, whereupon he said, "Why don't you come up in our office? We have a vacant room there because Clarence Hopkins has just left us. Come up there and run your own practice from there."

That chance meeting, or rather physical encounter, is really responsible for my connection with the firm. The room available for me in the office was entirely adequate and the office staff was available to me, and the expense of conducting my small law practice would, therefore, be much less. So it was that I became the occupant of that room in the office of Pennie, Davis & Goldsborough. From then on I conducted my little law practice there and had much occasion for wishing that my clientele was more numerous.

I had been working in the office there for several months when there came a time when Mr. Pennie walked into my room, probably the first time he had been in there during my occupancy. He wore a worried look and was hesitant about coming out with what he had on his mind. Finally he asked me if I could help him out of a predicament he found himself in. He

## My Entrance into the Pennie Davis Organization

explained that there was an interference proceeding which had progressed to the point of taking testimony, that he had postponed the introduction of proofs such a number of times that he could not postpone it further, and that he was so engaged on other matters it was quite impossible for him to arrange to take the testimony himself. He said the testimony would have to be taken at Grand Rapids, Michigan, that he could not go out there at that time, and that he wondered if I could go out there and take the testimony for him. He presented the subject as though I would be doing him a great personal favor if I would relieve him of the embarrassment growing out of this terrible jam he was in. He told me briefly what the situation was and who the people he represented were and said he would write a letter to them which would pave the way for me. It was with much difficulty that I suppressed an exhibition of the enthusiasm with which I welcomed this proposal, for my aspirations in the practice of patent law at that time far exceeded the needs of the small and select few whom I was wont to think of as my clients. To me this was just the thing I wanted to do, so I welcomed the opportunity and proceeded at once to study the applications involved.

I went out to Grand Rapids on the night train and in the morning presented myself at the office of Grand Rapids Veneer Works. What a cold reception I received! The President and Secretary, the active officers of the company, were terribly disappointed over not having the pleasure of welcoming Mr. Pennie and working with him. The letter Mr. Pennie had written, a fine letter I am sure, did not develop any warmth for my reception. After a long wait, I was allowed to go into the Secretary's room, and, after some further talk, I was allowed to meet the men who had to be the witnesses. There was nothing to do but make the best of the situation I found myself in, frigid as it was, and I made what progress I could with the men who had to be the witnesses.

The next morning my adversary arrived and we started taking testimony. From time to time the Secretary would look in on the proceedings and little by little he seemed to think I was proceeding acceptably. On the next day I was received with a slightly increased cordiality. More testimony was taken and a little greater satisfaction seemed to be apparent. Then the President appeared the next day. Along about the fourth day the President softened up to the point of taking me to his house for dinner, and, when I finished up at the end of the week, the President took me down to the railroad station. To all outward appearances he had gotten over his disappointment at not having Mr. Pennie there with him.

While the President, a Mr. Thwing, and I were at the station awaiting the arrival of my train, he told me that the City of Grand Rapids was growing rapidly as an industrial center, and, although it had already reached considerable size, there was no one practicing patent law in the whole of the city. Then he went on to say that it might be well for me to consider coming out to Grand Rapids to live and practice patent law there. He followed this by saying that if I concluded to do that, he would undertake to see that I met the heads of all of the industrial companies in and around Grand Rapids.

During the evening I spent with the President, he spoke of his admiration for Mr. Pennie but complained that the professional work for his company did not proceed as rapidly as he had hoped for. He went on to tell me of a competitor out there in Grand Rapids whom he wanted to sue for infringement of one of his patents and expressed regret that the suit had never been started. I had grown up in a law office where any failure to comply promptly with an expressed wish of a client would call

## My Entrance into the Pennie Davis Organization

forth a severe reprimand, if not something worse, so I was quick to assure this President that if he wanted a suit brought, I would see that it was brought forthwith, and in a very short time after my return to New York a complaint in the suit was filed.

Then pretty soon it became necessary for the other party to the interference to take testimony and Mr. Pennie was served with a notice of testimony to be taken in Detroit. Again he came around to me and said I would do him a great favor if I would attend the taking of testimony in Detroit. It was easy for me to accede to his request because it was just what I wanted to do.

I went to Detroit and the Secretary of the company met me there. We were kept waiting for a couple of hours in the office of Whittemore, Hulbert & Belknap, with no explanation whatever, and finally were told that the testimony would not be taken that morning and that we should come back at three o'clock. We appeared at three o'clock and again nothing happened for about an hour. Finally Mr. Belknap appeared and told us rather sheepishly that his client whose testimony he had proposed to take had gotten inordinately tight the night before, that efforts to resuscitate him all through the morning had failed and that he had decided, reluctantly but definitely, that no testimony at all would be taken. Back I came to New York on the night train.

Thus my effort to aid Mr. Pennie by taking charge of his interference for him scored a complete success, though hardly a great professional triumph.

Meanwhile the suit we had filed in Grand Rapids progressed through the usual stages and soon the case was set for trial. Again Mr. Pennie was engrossed in matters of importance to him and he found it impossible to go out to Grand Rapids to try the case. Discussions of this situation ended with the decision that Davis and I would go out there and try it.

This was shortly after the adoption of the new Equity Rules providing for the trial of patent suits in open court rather than by depositions taken out of court followed by oral argument and the filing of printed records and briefs. Practically no one in patent practice had had any experience qualifying him for such procedure, but Davis and I concluded that since we were no worse off than all the others, we would go out to Grand Rapids and do the best we could. We had a perfectly wonderful time. Our adversary was this same Mr. Belknap of Detroit and we performed better than he did by a large margin. Also, all the "breaks" came our way. Belknap's principal witness made himself vulnerable and on cross-examination he was quite thoroughly discredited; and we were able to get as fact witnesses one or two industrialists prominent in Grand Rapids who performed in our behalf quite admirably. Finally we reached the end of the trail and the Judge announced that he was prepared to decide the case then and there, and soon we were all seated in a big semicircle in front of the bench. Judge Sessions[7] discussed quite adequately and stated his views on each of the several issues presented and ended up with a decision in our favor. Our client, of course, was jubilant, and as for Davis and myself, our first act on getting out of the Court House was to go to a Western Union office and telegraph Mr. Pennie that we had won his case for him. On our return to the office he congratulated us and went on to say that maybe a good program would be for him to take out patents and for Davis and me to litigate them, and he added that if he did a good job of soliciting, our task of sustaining the patents would be much easier.

It was not very long after I took over this interference situation for Mr. Pennie that he got into another jam where something had to be done within a prescribed time and he could not

## My Entrance into the Pennie Davis Organization

do it. Again he came to me and again I took over the assignment with avidity and this went on through several such matters.

Through the balance of the year 1914, I said to Davis on two or three occasions that at some time they should tell me how much I owed the firm as rent for my quarters in the office and for stenographic assistance, etc. Davis, unlike myself, showed no interest in the topic; he said merely that something appropriate along that line would be done some time. As month after month went by, I became more and more concerned about the amount of my indebtedness and how I could contrive to dispose of it, for my anemic law practice was not remunerative beyond my needs outside the office. Time ran on and nothing happened except that my concern mounted steadily. In fact, nothing happened until well along in the year 1915. Then one day Davis came into my room with some papers in his hands, and, at a slow pace, he let me know that the accounts for the preceding year had at last been made up in full. My initial reaction was that I was about to receive some very bad news and would have to brace myself against the blow. Davis went on with the explanation of various items, all of which postponed the announcement of the figure which I dreaded, and I found it quite difficult to suppress an exhibition of my concern. In fact, it seemed to me that the figure would never be announced. But finally, to my great relief, Davis said that the result of it all was that the firm owed me a sum in the hundreds of dollars. Then it was as difficult for me to suppress an exhibition of relief as I had experienced before in suppressing my concern. Evidently the aggregate of the work I had done for the firm was more than I had realized.

# Some Events in the Years Following 1914

The professional work of the firm seemed to increase constantly and there had to be additions to the staff. Mr. Barrows[8] was the first addition. He came with us at some time in 1915. There was no room available for his use and he had to take a desk in the outer space just outside the door to Mr. Pennie's room.

Later one or two others were taken on and we were able to add to the office space two or three rooms on the Liberty Street side of the building just beyond Mr. Davis's room.

During 1915, Mr. Marvin was made a partner in the firm and the firm name was changed from Pennie, Davis & Goldsborough to Pennie, Davis & Marvin.

After I had taken on a number of matters like that interference for Mr. Pennie and had handled them to his satisfaction and also to his great relief, while continuing with my own practice, Mr. Pennie and Mr. Davis told me it seemed rather futile to continue under that program with my meager practice handled separately and that they thought a much better program would

## Some Events in the Years Following 1914

be for us to put all matters in one pot and for me to join the firm. That program commended itself to me and at some time, I think the first of 1917, this was carried out and the firm became Pennie, Davis, Marvin & Edmonds.

The firm continued to grow and obtaining more space was imperative and we were fortunate in being able to secure all of the remaining space on the thirteenth floor right there where we were. A floor plan of the office when so expanded is annexed. Mr. Davis was installed in the room at the corner and I had the room next to him on the Liberty Street side. Mr. Pennie took a room down in the middle on the Nassau Street side with Mr. Marvin and Mr. Barrows close to him.

Brown Morton[9] came with us at about that time and he took one of the rooms further along on the Liberty Street side and Sage[10] joined us too and occupied a room beyond Mr. Pennie's room.

We continued in these quarters for two or three years and then the building was bought by the Guaranty Trust Company whose bank building adjoined our building at the end of the Liberty Street wing. Guaranty was growing in a big way and had to have additional space and the purchase of our building was made with that in view. Unfortunately for us, we were notified that the bank had to have the thirteenth floor where we were established. We protested but the most we could accomplish was to get the sixth floor in the same building. We had to move down to that sixth floor and the quarters we had there were much inferior to those on the thirteenth floor, particularly as to the amount of daylight coming in at the windows. Obviously we would not want to stay there any great length of time and therefore we did not go very far in rearranging and redecorating on that floor.

With that in mind we looked around for other space, and, at

the end of one year on the sixth floor, we left 35 Nassau Street permanently. Over on Broadway at Cortlandt Street was the City Investing Building, a large building running all the way back to Church Street and twenty-six stories high with a tower of some four or five floors over part of it. When the building was built, space on the twenty-sixth floor was specially constructed to provide quarters appropriate for a downtown club and the City Lunch Club was organized with its headquarters there. It was done very elaborately; the Club quarters were handsome and comfortable and the membership included leaders in the business world in downtown New York. This continued until our country entered World War I, whereupon office space in downtown New York was in such demand for Government purposes that the Club was required to give up its space for Government occupancy. A war agency installed there continued in operation up through 1919 and approached the end of its activities at about the time when we began to look for a new office. Eventually we leased the space. It was a big undertaking to move from one building to another and to assume a rent way beyond what we had been paying.

There were other locations we had under consideration about the same time and I recall that on one Saturday we decided to meet at lunch at the Lawyers Club determined to settle the matter of new quarters without further delay. After adequate discussion over the lunch table, we all came to the view that the space at 165 Broadway was the best. The big obstacle was the amount of rent we had to pay. I put forward the view that it might be well to negotiate further in the effort to get a lower rent, but the others feared that during further negotiations somebody else might take the space. I told them that the negotiations I had in mind would be completed that afternoon, or at least on the next Monday morning. Accordingly it was agreed

## Some Events in the Years Following 1914

that I could do what negotiating I pleased so long as it did not cover more than that maximum length of time and I was to close the deal whether or not the negotiation achieved anything. One of them even went so far as to make a bet with me of a good cigar that I could not accomplish anything in further negotiating.

With that, our lunch meeting adjourned and I went at once to 165 Broadway. I had an interesting experience there, and within no more than an hour I was back at the office at 35 Nassau Street and informed those who were still there that the mission was accomplished, the deal was closed, and I had saved the firm $10,000 by getting a lease for $2,000 less for each of the five years of its term.

We did a good job of fixing up the new space to meet our needs; one large room was specially arranged for Mr. Pennie and I was given first choice of the space other than that room because of the deal I had made on the lease. I chose the room at the corner with windows looking south and west out over the Hudson River and New York Harbor, even though it was not as large as some of the other rooms.

One further matter relating to those years might well be mentioned. In the summer of 1916 I attended the Officers Training Camp at Plattsburg, New York, and when this country entered World War I, I fully expected to get into service. But professional work in the office was growing continually, particularly some parts that were under my care, and before I could make my suitable arrangement whereby I could go into service, Mr. Pennie took on some special assignments in connection with war work. This required considerable rearrangement of the conduct of professional work within the office and much of it devolved on me.

A little later, Mr. Davis accepted appointment under General

Goethals down in Washington in connection with Army contracts for supplies of any and all kinds. Off he went, withdrawing almost completely from our professional work while devoting himself to Army contracts under General Goethals in association with Goldthwaite Dorr of the New York Bar, Mr. Lehmann who later became Governor and Senator, and others who had responded to the call. This required another redistribution of professional work in the office and again this devolved on me. Even after the War was over, Davis's contract work in Washington continued for many months, and, in January of 1919, Mr. Pennie was invited to join the Peace Commission and he went over to Paris, leaving here on March 9, 1919. It was not until well along in 1919 that he was released from this service and came back to us to resume the law practice.

# THE BERLIN MILLS CASE

THE GREAT BERLIN MILLS CASE DECIDED FINALLY BY THE UNITED States Supreme Court has many interesting facets, and one of them that appeals to me relates to Mr. Barrows.

He had been in patent practice over in Washington for some years, most of his jobs being for out-of-town attorneys, pre-exes principally, and he has told me how he made pre-exes at $2.50 per. I think he had one client in the category known as "original clients". That one was a manufacturer of artificial limbs. In addition to his proficiency in the art of artificial limbs, Barrows's knowledge of the science of chemistry was profound and comprehensive, more so than that of most patent attorneys, even those specializing in that field.

In some way, these manifold capacities of the young Mr. Barrows came to the attention of Mr. Pennie. The result was that Barrows came over to New York and joined us at 35 Nassau Street along in 1915.

In those days, Barrows was a very mild-mannered, soft-spoken, reserved and studious individual and he continued to be so for months after he joined us. The metamorphosis which occurred then, the complete metamorphosis by which he became a pugnacious, belligerent, virulent and persistent advocate, was striking, and I had something to do with the change, which latter explains why it is that I include this reference to the transmogrification of Barrows.

The well-known Proctor & Gamble Company, prominent in soap manufacture, got around to making a lard substitute, using for the purpose cottonseed oil which it treated by a process of hydrogenation, and Proctor & Gamble obtained patents for the process and the product and proceeded with exploitation of artificial lard, Crisco by name, with conspicuous success.

Up north in New Hampshire and Maine was a company of considerable size operating under the name Berlin Mills, its primary activity being in the field of paper. In its paper manufacturing procedure, it produced a considerable amount of hydrogen and let this by-product pass out into the air. Then some bright individual suggested that this considerable quantity of hydrogen be utilized and that a good way to do it would be to hydrogenize cottonseed oil to produce an artificial lard compound. So Berlin Mills went into that business and before long it was sued by Proctor & Gamble, and a good friend of Mr. Pennie's over in Boston by the name of Marcus B. May took over the defense of Berlin Mills and sought Mr. Pennie's cooperation. Day after day these two men worked together, canvassing every phase of the situation presented in the suit.

When Barrows joined us, it was inevitable that he would get into the Berlin Mills case in a big way. After getting abreast of all that had occurred and making his own thorough study of the available literature, Barrows found himself rather nonplussed as to what to do next. He thought there were some measures that should be taken in the interest of the defendant but he did not seem to be able to ferret out what they were. After prolonged study along this line, he seemed to come to the view that it might be well to talk with others and see if he could not evolve some suggestion from such discussions. Proceeding on that course, he came in to my room to talk with me about the case. He described the situation presented in the suit at considerable length, and, in particular, those aspects of it which baffled him. After our discussion had covered the facts adequately and had developed the critical issues and the difficulties confronting us, I told him I thought he ought to go right into the camp of the enemy, that he should put on the witness stand any and all of the technical and business heads of Proctor & Gamble who might be made to impart to him some useful information on the points where he needed information, that in examining them he should be insistent upon getting fully responsive answers to all of his questions directed to points he thought important, and that, if they tried to hold out on him, he should go before the court and have them required to give full and frank answers. That gave him something to think about and didn't he do it!

Before long I learned that the heads of Proctor & Gamble had been subpoenaed and that Barrows was on his way to Cincinnati to engage in battle with them.

When Barrows came back from that trip, he was the belligerent, pugnacious, driving individual he has been ever since. The metamorphosis was complete. It all dates back to that Proctor & Gamble case. There and then he became the rip-roaring rampant he has been ever since.

The ensuing history of the Berlin Mills case may be stated briefly as follows:

Mr. Pennie tried the case before the District Court in New York, then operating in the Woolworth Building. He tried it very well indeed and in his presentation he was very impressive. Also, his oral argument was persuasive and the District Court upheld all of his contentions. An appeal was taken by the plaintiff and eminent members of the Bar were drawn into the case in its behalf. Briefs were submitted to the Court of Appeals and there was an oral argument, and, to our great dismay, the Court of Appeals reversed (256 Fed. Rep. 23).[11] That was a devastating blow and Messrs. Pennie, May and Barrows were cast into a gloom the depth and murkiness of which they had never known before. Then there was the inevitable consideration of applying for <u>certiorari</u>. But the prospect offered by that was none too favorable. Because of that, much thought was given to anything and everything that might prove helpful and eventually the big idea was achieved. There had been a presidential election not long prior to that and Charles Evans Hughes had resigned from the office of Associate Justice of the Supreme Court to become a candidate for the Presidency. He failed of election with the result that he was neither President nor Supreme Court Justice, and, being in need of occupation and possibly of some money too, he went back to his earlier occupation of practicing law. The big idea was to bring him into the case in behalf of Berlin Mills and that was done, and he was largely responsible for the preparation of a very persuasive petition for certiorari, but the big item was that his name appeared on the petition at the head of the long list of counsel representing the petitioner.

    The petition, of course, went to his former associates on the Bench, and they, possibly thinking the reconstituted private practitioner might be in need of professional employment, granted the petition. Mr. Hughes took the case on as a major effort. He studied it to the point of mastering it, and, when it came on for hearing, he presented an impressive argument which convinced his former associates and secured the reversal which saved Berlin Mills from final defeat, and, what is more important to us, restored the equanimity and indeed the faith of Messrs. Pennie, May and Barrows. (254 U.S. 156).[12]

# Wireless Telegraphy

It was back in those years prior to 165 Broadway that we got into wireless telegraphy in a big way. Davis got started with it when he worked for years on the Marconi patents while in the office of Betts, Sheffield & Betts. Long after that, around 1913, he came to know about Armstrong, then a student at Columbia University, who had come to the notice of Professor Morton Arendt of Columbia, a friend of Mr. Davis. Armstrong came to our office and Davis took out various patents for him, including his great patent, the patent for the so-called Armstrong feedback or regenerative circuit. Davis litigated the patent against Lee De Forest and battled with De Forest very effectively indeed when the latter took the stand as the principal witness in his own behalf. Davis scored a great victory. Armstrong was held to be the inventor of the circuit, the spurious pretensions of De Forest were rejected, and the patent in suit was sustained. Appeal was to be expected but at that point the Westinghouse company decided to acquire some important patent assets in the wireless field and it bought the Armstrong patent and also some Fessenden patents which had important possibilities. These patent assets were used by Westinghouse in its tight competition with G.E. in the wireless field, out of which came the formation of the Radio Corporation of America, owned in large part by G.E. and Westinghouse by reason of their assignment of valuable patent rights to R.C.A.

In that period back in 1914 and 1915 when I was doing the best I could with a feeble patent practice of my own, I took on the representation of some men who had been joined personally as defendants in a patent suit in the wireless field which terminated adverse to their interests, with the result that they personally were enjoined. I expended much effort in trying to better the situation for them and made some little progress, though the remuneration which I received for my efforts was minute by reason of the low state of their resources. Though I got such a meager financial return, from time to time they sent others to me and those others were much more remunerative. One of them was a young man named Grebe who incorporated himself as the A.H. Grebe Company and we did a considerable amount of patent work for that company. Mr. Taylor[13] had joined us by that time and he took this over.

Another situation which they sent to me was of far greater moment.

Up to a time in 1914, there had been no commercial transatlantic wireless telegraphy. Then the great Telefunken interests in Germany thought they had developed wireless to the point where transatlantic service on a commercial basis was possible and Telefunken formed a company in this country under the name Atlantic Communication Company to take charge of the American end of the effort which Telefunken proposed to make. Atlantic was financed and proceeded to build a wireless station at Sayville, Long Island, and Telefunken and Atlantic entered into an agreement governing the distribution of all moneys received by Atlantic for transmitting transoceanic messages by wireless. This agreement was known as the "Traffic Agreement" and later became the subject of sharp controversy. The Sayville station was built and persistent efforts were made to transmit messages back and forth with Telefunken. Sporadic signals came through, particularly at night, so they knew they were on the edge of achievement, but nothing approaching satisfactory operation emerged. Then after the top talent at Sayville had tried every expedient they could think of with no encouraging results, so much so that they were completely baffled, someone spoke of a young man by the name of Armstrong at Columbia University who had devised something which had received approving comment and put forward the suggestion that this obscure Mr. Armstrong be approached. With nothing else to do that offered any promise, Armstrong was communicated with and then invited to come to Sayville, and before long Armstrong's feedback circuit was incorporated in the Sayville circuit. Almost at once the operation was improved and soon the Sayville station was operating successfully and commercial transatlantic radio became an accomplished fact for the first time in history.

With the cables to Europe put out of commission as a war measure, the Sayville Telefunken wireless service became the only service of rapid communication with Germany and it was utilized in a big way. The receipts, when divided between Atlantic and Telefunken as specified in the Traffic Agreement, gave Atlantic a considerable revenue.

Then early in 1917 this country entered the War and immediately seized the Sayville station. The service of the station was continued but under thoroughgoing Government control. American technicians were put in the plant to operate it, and the staff of German technicians who had built and operated it were released, most of them going back to Germany.

Long prior to this, the owners of the Fessenden patents had brought two suits for infringement against Atlantic. The suits had been tried in the District Court and the patents had been sustained. As usual, this developed much dissatisfaction of the German officers of Atlantic with the patent counsel who had represented them and had lost both of their cases. Atlantic had to seek other patent counsel and these friends of mine to whom I have referred were responsible for directing Atlantic to me. The official of Atlantic who represented the company in dealings with me told me it had been decided by Atlantic that no appeals would be taken in the two patent cases referred to, that accounting proceedings would be allowed to go ahead, and that later on when final decrees were entered, then consideration would be given to taking appeals. These were definite instructions to me, the obvious explanation being that, in the war conditions then prevailing, any measures that would extend over a considerable period of time might well be adopted. On examining into the situation I found that in addition to these two suits against Atlantic on the Fessenden patents, already decided against Atlantic, there was another suit brought by Marconi against Atlantic based upon the De Forest patent for the three-element tube which had already been sustained in another litigation. To make the situation worse for my side, I found myself in the position of having no technical assistance available to me because, with the seizure of the Sayville station, the technical staff which had built and operated it had disintegrated. This was quite a predicament, but I mention it only because of what ensued.

When the Alien Property Custodian took over the Sayville plant, I was asked to continue to represent Atlantic in these three suits and I consented to do so, and soon I found myself served with notices that the plaintiff in the suits on the Fessenden patents proposed to proceed with the accounting in which the Court had appointed as Master the Honorable E. Henry Lacombe, who had been a Judge of the United States Circuit Court in New York and had retired after many years of distinguished service.

I attended the introduction of plaintiff's proofs in the accounting and cross-examined as best I could. The outstanding thing about plaintiff's proofs was that plaintiff asserted a claim to <u>all</u> of the profits of the Sayville station on the ground that the use of its patented inventions had been essential to successful operation. Finally the introduction of testimony came to an end and I was notified that plaintiff's accounting proofs were closed. The next move was up to me.

After much deliberation, I went around to see Mr. L.F.H. Betts of Betts, Sheffield & Betts, representing Marconi in the suit against Atlantic on the De Forest patent which had been sustained. I told Mr. Betts that, subject to two conditions, I would give him a decree by consent. That rather amazed him but he recovered enough to inquire what were the two conditions. I told him that one of them was that I be allowed to name the Master in the accounting proceeding. He said before agreeing to that he would have to know who I would name. I told him I would name the Honorable E. Henry Lacombe. He responded at once that that condition was acceptable and asked what the other one was. I told him the other condition was that in the accounting proceeding pursuant to the decree to which I would consent, he would have to introduce <u>prima facie</u> proofs within a limited period, say six weeks, and he said that condition was acceptable. A decree was entered and Hon. E. Henry Lacombe was named as the Master.

Not long after that we had sessions before Judge Lacombe at which Marconi introduced its proofs and in those proofs Marconi claimed that it was entitled to all the profits because the use of its patented invention as essential to successful operation. The attorneys representing the Fessenden patents had been allowed to participate in these proceedings and they proceeded to cross-examine the plaintiff's witnesses in an effort to depreciate to the limit the value and importance of the De Forest patent. In repelling this effort of the attorneys for the Fessenden patents, the Marconi witnesses presented scathing comments on the so-called inventions of the Fessenden patents and so it was that these two plaintiffs, both pursuing Atlantic, were drawn into controversy with each other with each trying with all its skill and its best technicians to tear down all of the contentions of the other. I, who had no technical assistance at all, could sit there and listen with much satisfaction, restraining myself as best I could from applauding the efforts of both plaintiffs and waiting my turn to reply to both of them.

When the two attorneys had done their worst to each other and my time to introduce testimony came on, all of my testimony was directed to explaining the Traffic Agreement, why its provisions were entirely fair, how they had been applied in the division of Atlantic's receipts, and so forth, with the result that the sum remaining available for distribution to any and all patentees whose patents had been used was of a limited amount, something under $100,000. This, in brief, was the situation presented at the end of the introduction of proofs.

Shortly thereafter, Judge Lacombe rendered his decision. He observed that each of the two plaintiffs could not be given all of the profits, as each had claimed as its due, and he followed this with a decision that two-thirds of what was available should go to the owners of the Fessenden patents and one-third to the owner of the De Forest patent; and he upheld the Traffic Agreement as a binding agreement which was so fair in its terms under the circumstances that it could not be set aside on the ground that it was part of a scheme to divert profits improperly. On this basis, the amounts which the two plaintiffs could collect were less than amounts which I had offered them in settlement, and they were furious, particularly the attorney representing the Fessenden patents who branded Judge Lacombe's opinion as an "outrage".

Then we all went to the District Court for affirmance of the Master's decision and there we got before Judge Julius Mayer. He reviewed the whole case and set aside the Traffic Agreement, thereby making some sum like one-half million dollars available for payments to the two plaintiffs. But he went on to say that a new allocation of the profits had to be made because there were other patents to be considered additional to the three on which the pending suits were based, namely, the patents for all of the inventions which had to be used in order to achieve success in transatlantic wireless. That led to a most interesting proceeding before the District Court presided over by Judge Mayer. It was a symposium of the views of various men of distinction in the wireless art of that day as to what were the inventions essential to success and their relative values. Judge Mayer's decision in this interesting proceeding appears in 51 Fed.2, 109.[14]

That, of course, was a severe defeat for our client, the U.S.A. represented by the Alien Property Custodian, and an appeal was in order. The appeal came on to be heard before the Court of Appeals and the proceedings at the argument had some elements of interest. On the appeal, Marconi was represented by Mr. Sheffield, of Betts, Sheffield & Betts, who had then returned to his firm after being Ambassador to Mexico. He would have done better had he stayed in Mexico, or if he had addressed his fellow Republicans at the Republican Club. He did not succeed in engaging the attention of the Judges of the Court of Appeals at all and when I started to tell the Court about the Traffic Agreement and how fair it was and what resulted from application of its terms, they took it all in with much interest. The end of it was that the Court of Appeals reversed the District Court (290 Fed. 698)[15] and reinstated the decision of the Master, and the two plaintiffs got awards in amounts less than they had paid out in litigation expenses, amounts which were about what I had offered them in settlement years before.

These several proceedings including the litigation of Armstrong's patent rights and settlement of the claims against Atlantic Communication Company marked the early stages of our activities in the radio art. Along in them, Mr. Taylor came with us after he got out of service in World War I and along with him came Prof. Hazeltine and Neutrodyne and a host of others leading up to the big battle of recent years in behalf of Zenith against R.C.A.

# The Bessemerization of Copper

BACK IN THE DAYS WHEN BUTTE, MONTANA, WAS A SEETHING cauldron of copper mining, political intrigue and labor strifes, there was a Norwegian by the name of E.A. Cappelen Smith out there who improved the converting of copper matte by devising what has since been known as the basic-lined copper converter. When he was convinced that success had been attained and thought he had made an invention and was entitled to a patent, he sought the assistance of a firm of patent attorneys in Chicago. These attorneys struggled with the assignment over an extended period of time and with diligent application, but they were never able to produce anything that satisfied either them or Cappelen Smith. Finally they told Smith that what the conditions called for was a "process patent attorney" and that he should authorize them to secure the services of someone in that category. Smith agreed and they came to New York and consulted Mr. Pennie. They could not have made a better choice; Mr. Pennie had all of the qualifications which they lacked — all they thought of as distinguishing the "process patent attorney". Mr. Pennie did what was appropriate, and one result of his efforts was the Smith patent No. 943,280 of December 14, 1909. Other results were the enduring gratitude to and veneration of Mr. Pennie by Cappelen Smith and his Chicago attorneys.

The patented Smith process was put into use under license at smelters of American Smelting and Refining and Anaconda and others and Smith acquired wealth and recognition as an outstanding metallurgist and high status in the Guggenheim officialdom. But some of the copper companies held out and it appeared that litigation would be necessary and one substantially contemporaneous effort in this same field was threatening. I spent about six weeks of the summer of 1916 investigating the facts about this rival effort at Butte and Anaconda. Finally we brought suit in behalf of Peirce-Smith Converter Company against United Verde Copper Company in the Delaware District Court.

I was associated with Mr. Pennie during the early stages of this suit as an outgrowth of the investigation I had made in Montana in 1916, and in the preliminary proceedings I had many contacts with a Mr. Blackman, representing the defendant. One time along about the first of December of, I think, 1919, Mr. Blackman came over to see me and told me that, by reason of a tax situation in United Verde, the company could afford to offer a considerable sum in the settlement of the suit provided the settlement could be completed and the money paid before the end of the year. After much discussion, the offered payment became $350,000. That seemed to me to be a large sum and it was a large sum in those days; and, having in mind the uncertainties of litigation, I was inclined to look with favor on the settlement. Out of this came a meeting in Mr. Pennie's room with various people there including Cappelen Smith and several representatives of United Verde. The offer of a settlement was made and discussed in much detail, but throughout the discussion Mr. Pennie and Cappelen Smith seemed to me to become more and more dejected and dispirited and altogether low in their minds. Finally the meeting adjourned and I was left there with Mr. Pennie and Cappelen Smith. They seemed to have no interest in the proposed settlement. The offer of a money payment had no appeal. Finally Cappelen Smith made it plain that what he wanted was a decree of a court saying that he was the inventor of basic-lined copper converters and nothing less than that would satisfy him regardless of how much money was involved. Mr. Pennie seemed to be of a like frame of mind, namely, that he wanted to have a court pass on that patent which was his handiwork and represented his effort to secure patent protection for Cappelen Smith's monumental achievement.

Many things happened after that to retard the progress of the litigation, primarily Mr. Pennie's trip to Paris on the Peace Commission, and absorption of others in war work and the aftermath of the war. Then Mr. Pennie passed away.

Mr. Davis took over the responsibility for the suit and he brought in Mr. Gifford of Gifford & Bull in behalf of the plaintiff, along with Jack Neary of Wilmington, Delaware, and our Mr. Sage, and the case came on for trial down in Wilmington before Judge Morris. Gifford was terribly bearish about the prospect and stated frankly to Davis that he thought there was no chance of getting the patent sustained. Principally by reason of this, Davis took over all of the activities in behalf of the plaintiff at the trial. By the time he had finished the presentation of voluminous <u>prima facie</u> proofs, he had built up such a convincing case in support of the patent that even the pessimist Gifford reversed himself completely and told Davis that he had an impregnable case. Judge Morris seemed to think so too and he sustained the patent and held it infringed (293 Fed. 108),[16] and held it valid and infringed again (298 Fed. 763)[17] after re-opening for some so-called newly-discovered evidence. Also the Court of Appeals for the Third Circuit affirmed (7 F.(2d) 13).[18]

In the final settlement, United Verde paid Peirce Smith a big round sum, two or three times the amount that had been offered in settlement.

\* \* \* \* \*

These three lines of our professional work I have commented on at some length because Mr. Pennie was the active head of the defense in the Berlin Mills case and saw it through to a successful finish, he took out the Smith patent and started the suit on it and formulated the plan for all that was done later, and he was with us during about eight years of our early work in the wireless field. Also he was responsible for, or had something to do with, a number of other lines of work the firm pursued, including some that we have gone along with right up to the present day. To some of them I shall refer later. But, at this point, I come to the sad event of 1921.

# Mr. Pennie was Taken from Us

It was on May 1, 1920, that we moved from 35 Nassau Street to 165 Broadway, twenty-sixth floor. It was a big office, in a big building, with a Broadway address, and an imposing Broadway entrance. Up on high in the building was our office, larger and far more imposing than what we had before, and made the more imposing because the large open central space had the high domed ceiling provided for the super-de-luxe lunch-club of former years. In this fine new setting, The Chief, as I called him, had a commodious room well suited to him and fulfilling his every wish. He was a little past sixty, in the full vigor of mature life, an imposing figure, always busy but never too busy for a kind word and a humorous comment. He could look back with satisfaction on an extended period of national service in a major role in the war effort. And around him was quite a group of vigorous younger men, working hard and, he thought, working well, but all of them ready at any minute to drop anything they were doing if they could do anything for him.

He could, and did, view the situation before him with much satisfaction. He was the senior partner in a law firm of considerable size and with an established position in the business and professional world. The firm had a fine office, well located and well adapted to its needs. And in it was a staff that satisfied him, devoted to him and devoted to the high principles of the profession that he had always maintained.

The whole setting pleased him very much. He felt that he had attained the fulfillment of what he had been striving for in his professional life, and he had attained it while he was in his early sixties and could look forward to ten or more years of the professional work he loved in a setting which seemed to him to be so eminently satisfactory.

So it went for a time — for all too short a time — for a little over a year. Then things started going badly. Then there was a terribly bad week, and, at the end of it, Mr. Pennie was gone. That was in December, 1921.

That was a sad blow for all of us. But there was nothing to do but carry on — carry on as he would have us carry on and in the tradition we had absorbed from him.

We did carry on and among the many lines of professional work which Mr. Pennie started and we carried on are a couple that might well have a passing comment.

# Air Reduction Company

Airco[19] was formed about 1916 to commercialize operations in separating air into its components, a procedure which had been the subject of much research by a small organization financed by the founders of Airco. Also, Airco took over the American rights of a French company named "L'air Liquide" which had done much research work in this same field and we had been the U.S. patent solicitors for this French company. That, and possibly also the years of friendship of Mr. Pennie and one of the top chemists in the Airco group, led to Mr. Pennie being brought into the picture as the company's patent counsel. In those early years of its existence, Airco had a small office in the Equitable Building, just around the block from our office at 35 Nassau Street. About that time we took on Ernest Merchant as a member of our staff, and then it was arranged that Merchant would spend half of each working day in our office on the firm's general practice and the other half in the Airco office on patent work for Airco. This arrangement continued for years, long after we moved to 165 Broadway, and after Airco, then grown to considerable size, moved uptown to 342

Madison Avenue. Merchant did the patent soliciting, and Mr. Pennie did what supervisory work was needed, mostly in conference with his friend Dr. Metzger of Airco.

Then along in the early twenties, one of the Airco applications got into an interference and a vast amount of testimony was taken on both sides. Merchant was so confident that he had things well in hand and was going to win with ease that all of us, busily engaged on other work, left it entirely to him. He went down to Washington for the final hearing before the Examiner of Interferences, still supremely confident of an easy victory. But he came back in a very different frame of mind and before long we received an adverse decision. It caused quite a bit of consternation in the Airco management because by that time the invention in controversy had assumed considerable importance.

Then one day when Merchant came downtown from a morning in the Airco office, he came in to me and told me that Airco wanted an independent opinion as to the prospect on appeal, that is, the opinion of someone in our firm who had had no connection with the interference up to that time. Accordingly, I tried to get Davis or Marvin or someone else to take on the assignment, but all of them explained that they were crowded right up to the limit. So, as in other such cases, I took on the job myself, though I was as crowded as the others.

The record in the interference was enormous and the briefs were of considerable volume and what soon appeared to be the critical issue was a close one, so the job I took on was a laborious one admitting of no shortcuts.

Eventually I concluded that, on the close critical issue, Airco had the better case and I wrote this conclusion into an opinion which ended with the recommendation that an appeal be taken, supplementing this with the statement that on appeal I thought Airco should win.

Merchant took this opinion to Airco where it was read by some of the officers and, before the lapse of many days, he came to me on his return from Airco and told me that the Airco people had noted that I recommended an appeal and thought Airco should win on appeal and that Airco had instructed him to tell me to appeal the case, and win it.

The appeal was taken, the case was briefed and argued and we did win. However, the procedure at the time provided for another appeal, and, because of the closeness of the case, I had to realize that much risk attended that further appeal. In connection with these proceedings, I had occasion to see the opposing attorney from time to time and, in the course of discussions with him, I evolved a plan of settlement much to Airco's advantage which I thought I could get the other side to agree to. Accordingly, I had a session with the President of Airco at which the situation was canvassed and the conference ended with him telling me that if I could settle the whole controversy in accordance with the plan I had outlined, Airco would welcome it. The settlement was made and it removed a considerable hazard to further growth of Airco.

By that time Mr. Pennie had passed away, and, from then on, I had to take on all of the Airco matters which were beyond the soliciting function performed by Merchant. We had a number of suits which were tried and we were successful in all but one of them. I recall one that was tried before Judge Learned Hand, then a District Court Judge, which ended not only successfully but also dramatically. It was a suit against Airco for patent infringement and it was critical for plaintiff to establish an early date for the so-called invention of the patent in suit. The plaintiff's effort on this point was amateurish and included the offer in evidence of a drawing on tracing cloth, the glaze of which had obviously been scraped off at the area where the date appeared.

At the end of the one-day trial, the plaintiff's attorney presented an oral argument at the close of which he made some attempt at a peroration which he concluded with something like "And for these reasons I think the patent in suit should be sustained." At that point the trial came to an abrupt end. Judge Hand said, "Well, I don't agree with you. Bill dismissed," whereupon His Honor arose, obviously in a state of great indignation, gathered his robe around him, turned abruptly and stomped out of the courtroom, down the hall and into his private room, slamming the door behind him and leaving all of us in the courtroom speechless. Before anyone broke the silence, we heard the same loud steps coming down the corridor and Judge Hand re-entered the room and mounted the bench, with all of us wondering what was to come next. Then, in a stentorian tone, he said, "Mr. Clark, I order that Exhibit No. Blank be impounded. Do you understand? Impounded." With that he stalked out of the courtroom again with the same loud majestic tread while silence reigned in the room until we heard the door of the Judge's private office close again with the same loud bang.

After some years, Airco bought the Davis-Bournonville Company, a large manufacturer of cutting and welding torches, and with the company we took over a suit it had brought. It was the suit which eventually went to the United States Supreme Court.

That suit was based on three patents initially and they were very meager patents; one of them was a patent for putting two holes where before there had been but one. We sustained two of the patents in the District Court, got an affirmance in the Court of Appeals and lost one of the two in the Supreme Court, but, in the ensuing accounting proceeding, we collected what we thought was exactly the same amount we would have recovered if all three patents had been sustained.

# The Fuller Companies

BACK IN THE YEARS BEFORE WORLD WAR I, THERE WAS A VERY wonderful individual known as Colonel Fuller up in the Allentown-Catasauqua region, who had gotten along pretty well with the development of two companies known as the Fuller-Lehigh Company and the Fuller Engineering Company. His companies developed to the point of needing the services of patent attorneys and on that subject he consulted Dr. Richards[20] of Lehigh University and Dr. Richards was a devoted friend and admirer of Mr. Pennie. In that way, the patent matters of the Fuller companies were brought into the office back there at 35 Nassau Street. Much of the work related to powdered coal and that did not seem to intrigue Mr. Pennie, with the result that the patent affairs of the company in our office did not get the attention they should have had. I talked with Mr. Davis about this once or twice and he told me, based on his years of experience, that if I spoke to Mr. Pennie about it, he would merely say that he was hoping to reach these Fuller matters soon and would try to do so, but if I just took all of the papers out of the stack of papers on his desk and did something myself, or got someone else to do it, Mr. Pennie would certainly not resent it and almost undoubtedly would be profusely grateful.

After the lapse of more time, with nothing done for the Fuller interests, I collected all the papers in Mr. Pennie's absence and took them out of his room. I was working under pressure then and it seemed to me that Mr. Marvin was not, so I took the papers to Marvin, and, after canvassing them with him, he said he would take over all of the Fuller matters. However, more months went by with insufficient accomplishment for the Fuller companies, so I took the papers back from Marvin and proceeded with them myself and from that time on for many years I looked after Colonel Fuller's affairs which grew steadily in volume and importance.

Among them was an interference relating to burning powdered coal in the furnace of a boiler, a three-sided interference in which all three parties took testimony in great volume. One of the interested parties was the Hanna Company of Cleveland.[21] The Hanna attorney took a great mass of testimony in a room of the Hanna Company's office in Cleveland. The crux of the testimony was that Hanna had been the first to succeed in burning powdered fuel in the furnace of a large boiler and the date when this great event occurred was given by the Hanna applicant and corroborated by one or more others. It so happened, however, that I and the attorney for the third party noted a framed picture hanging on the wall of the room in which the testimony was taken. It showed a large boiler including the boiler tubes and the furnace under them and down under it was a burned match stuck upon the mat of the picture and under it was printed, "This is the match used to light the fuel for the first successful burning of powdered coal in the furnace of a boiler." Under that inscription was a date and the date was <u>subsequent</u> to the date given by the Hanna applicant as the date of his first reduction to practice! The case of the Hanna applicant did not thrive after that.

Colonel Fuller's purpose was to develop the powdered fuel business up to a point where it assumed impressive proportions and then sell it to one or the other of the two big competing companies, namely, Combustion Engineering and Babcock & Wilcox. The price became fixed at $4,000,000. Combustion wanted to buy it at that price but wanted to pay a substantial part of the purchase price with Combustion stock. This did not appeal to the Colonel so he went to Babcock & Wilcox, told them they should be in the powdered fuel business, and said that his company was for sale, that the price was $4,000,000 and that they could buy it at that price if they acted quickly, otherwise he would sell it to their competitor, Combustion. The deal was arranged with surprising alacrity, and one morning when I was sitting at my desk in 165 Broadway, Colonel Fuller came into the office, passed the telephone girl, came into my room without being announced, walked up to my desk, and, without saying a word, leaned over and put a check for $4,000,000 down in front of me.

In consummating this sale, the Colonel had reserved rights in what was known as the Kinyon pump[22] for all purposes other than the pumping of powdered coal, and the present Fuller Company for which we have been doing patent work for about thirty years is the company which he started, following the Babcock & Wilcox sale, to exploit the Kinyon pump for pumping grain, cement and anything else other than coal.

# Radium Luminous Paint

Back around 1920, an importer of Swiss watches under the name Hipp. Didisheim & Company[23] was sued for infringement of a patent purporting to cover the application of radium luminous paint to the hands and dials of watches and clocks. Something or somebody led them to put the defense of the suit in my hands. It would not have been a very formidable suit had it not been for one unusual circumstance. Back prior to World War I, this same Hipp. Didisheim & Company had imported a few Swiss watches with radium paint on the hands and dials and had been sued for infringement of this same patent, and, thinking the matter of little importance and of no future promise, submitted to a consent decree and proceeded to forget about this experience entirely. But World War I and the presence of American soldiers in Continental Europe brought about a popularity of radium luminous watches far beyond anything previously anticipated, and when the importers in New York began to import and sell such watches, Didisheim went along with the rest, forgetting entirely about the first suit, then some five or more years back in the pre-war past.

In the second suit, that consent decree was pleaded and we had to recognize it as a formidable obstacle, but we did the best we could and we were favored by a great piece of luck. The case came on for trial before a Federal District Judge from Wisconsin who was holding a patent term in New York to help out here. To him, the former consent decree was a big item and he did not seem to look with favor upon anything we presented in behalf of the defendant. We finally got to the end of the trial in a rather low state of mind about our prospects and the Judge told us that he was going back to Wisconsin and that both sides could write briefs and send them to him and then he would hand down his decision. In saying this, he did not seem to leave much doubt in anybody's mind as to how he was going to decide the case and our prospects were about as meager as they could be. However, both sides wrote briefs and sent copies out there to the Judge, but, at about the time our briefs arrived there, His Honor was taken sick, and, in a rather short time, he departed this life without having given any attention to our case.

The situation was reported to the District Court here and it was decided that we should print the record and present it and our briefs to Judge Julius Mayer, then on the District Court bench, and we would have an oral argument before him, whereupon he would file an opinion announcing his decision. We followed this course and our prospects took a decided upward turn because Judge Mayer seemed to think well of all the arguments we presented, as much so as the Wisconsin Judge had thought they were deficient. Judge Mayer decided the case in our favor (279 Fed. Rep. 601)[24] and the Court of Appeals affirmed (279 Fed. Rep. 1016).[25] If anyone in charge of a patent litigation finds himself and his client embarrassed by a former consent decree, I recommend that he make use of

Lawrence Mfg. Co. v. Janesville, 138 U.S. 552. It pulled us through in that Radium case.

The defense of this suit of American Radium Company vs. Didisheim was assumed by a group consisting of importers of Swiss watches, American manufacturers of watches and United States Radium Corporation[26] which made radium luminous paint and applied it to watch hands and dials or sold it to others for that use. I got to know the United States Radium officers very well in the course of the suit, and, after the successful outcome, they asked me to go on their Board of Directors, and years later, on the demise of two of my predecessors, I became Chairman of the Board, an office which I have held for about twenty-five years, during which the firm has served as the company's patent counsel.

During the first six or eight years of my official connection with U.S. Radium, its President was Mr. Arthur Roeder and a close friendship developed between us. When he left U.S. Radium, he became President of Colorado Fuel and Iron Corporation[27] at Denver, Colorado. After he had been there a short time, we became patent counsel for that company and have continued in that capacity ever since, even though Mr. Roeder gave up the presidency many years ago.

# Oxyacetylene Welding and American Metal Products Company

Back in the early nineteen-twenties and after I had taken over the direction of Airco's patent matters, with Merchant doing all of the soliciting work, there were a number of small companies engaged in making steel tubing by rolling steel strip into a tube and welding the seam with the oxyacetylene torch, and most of them bought their torches and the gases used with them from Airco. Also, at that time, there was a company named Elyria Iron & Steel Company out in Elyria, Ohio, which owned a considerable number of patents relating to the manufacture of steel tubing by that procedure, and Elyria thought its patents dominated the operation. Elyria brought a suit out in Cleveland against a small Ohio manufacturer based upon seven of its patents.

This small Ohio concern knew the others engaged in this same line of work and promptly told them that it was in no position to contest a patent suit with Elyria, and, if left on its own, it would make the best settlement it could and then Elyria would sue the others one after another. This brought about a couple of meetings of representatives of the various companies but their discussions at these meetings got them nowhere. Then a third and final meeting was arranged at a hotel in Detroit and Airco, the principal supplier of the torches and gases, was asked to attend the meeting. One of the Airco officials told me about this and an Airco engineer was selected to attend the meeting and he was sent down to me for instructions as to what he should do at the meeting.

A couple of days before the date of the meeting, the President of Airco called me on the phone and said he thought this engineer could not represent Airco appropriately at the meeting because the discussion there would be concerned primarily with patent litigations, and he went on to say it would be far better for me to attend in behalf of Airco. The result was that I went out to the meeting and on the night train with me were representatives of two companies which could be charged with infringement.

At the meeting the next morning, there was much discussion for about an hour which got nowhere at all, and then one of the these men who was on the train the night before told the meeting that they were not getting anywhere because no one who had spoken knew anything about patent litigations. Then he went on to say that there was one man present who could tell them something about such litigations and that he thought it would be well to listen to him. That pushed me into the picture and I told them what I thought they should know and how they could, if they wanted to, combine in the defense of the suit which had been brought so as to make it a test suit serving the interests of all, and I told them that if they did so combine and selected patent counsel who were capable of handling the situation properly, Airco would join with them in defending the suit.

Within a very short time after that, they adopted the program I had laid out for them and asked me to take charge of the defense. I drew up a short agreement covering the joint participation in the suit and it was signed at once by representatives of a dozen of the companies and later it was signed by some four or five others whose representatives at the meeting said they were not empowered to sign.

After much testimony by deposition, we got to trial at Cleveland with the plaintiff represented by Mr. Neave. Early in the trial, Mr. Neave withdrew the charge of infringement of four of the seven patents named in the complaint and the trial proceeded on the three remaining ones, and, in his brief following the trial, he withdrew one of those three. On the remaining two, our contentions were all sustained (15 F.2d, 106).[28] The plaintiff appealed and we had an argument before the Court of Appeals in Cincinnati, and there we got an affirmance, but Mr. Neave's mellifluous presentation registered with one of the Judges and led him to file a dissenting opinion (15 F.2d 111).[29]

One of the companies interested in this litigation and participating in the expense of the defense was a small company in Detroit controlled and operated by a young man by the name of Frederick C. Matthaei.[30] He took more interest in developments in the suit than any one of the others participating in the defense, so much so that he was present at the trial and he attended the argument in the Court of Appeals at Cincinnati. One result was that I got to know him very well and was much impressed with his ability and dynamic energy. Before we left Cincinnati after the argument, he told me of a friend of his who had invested in his little company and who wanted to get his money out to put it into a business of his own, and Matthaei said he would like to have me buy that stock and thus become a partner in his enterprise. I was so impressed with his drive and acumen that I thought it inevitable he would get somewhere in the business world and that I might do well to join up with him. So I bought this stock which he said was available. The company was then a small one and the investment was not large, but the automobile business was then small and it seemed likely to me that a well-managed small company might do pretty well in the process of growing up with the industry.

American Metal Products Company, under the leadership of Fred Matthaei, has grown steadily from that time back in the twenties to the present day. After it got to a size such that we though we should have more than one officer, Fred Matthaei's father and I were made Vice-Presidents of the company, and I have continued to be a Vice-President and Director to the present day. Fred Matthaei has been one of my close personal friends ever since, and he has proven to be all of the able industrialist I thought he was going to be back there in the early twenties.

# Enlarging Clientele

RECALLING INCIDENTS IN THE LITIGATION OF PATENTS FOR WELDING the seams of tubes brings to mind some incidents bearing on the clientele of a law firm, more particularly how to increase its clientele. Good friends, particularly good friends in high places, are very helpful to that end, and, for a firm practicing patent law, members of large law firms in general practice rate high as such valuable friends. Good examples of this are James McV. Breed of Breed, Abbott & Morgan, my intimate friend through forty-five years, and his older brother, William C. Breed, who founded the firm, and his nephew, William C. Breed, Jr., son of the founder and now one of the senior partners in the firm.

Another most excellent procedure, effective beyond all others, is to perform creditably, or even better than creditably, with the professional work that one undertakes; in particular do a better job than the adversary in a contested matter, and, if it is a suit in a court, get a favorable decision. In this category, it is especially gratifying to defeat the adversary in a patent litigation and then have the adversary come around and ask you to take over his professional work. We have had experiences of that kind, and one of them grew out of that tube-welding litigation.

The patents relating to welding the seams of tubes with the oxyacetylene torch were, as I have stated, owned by Elyria Iron & Steel Company, and Elyria also owned another group of patents relating to welding the seams of tubes electrically, using alternating current and making what was known as a "stitch-weld", the metal of the welded tube having minute slanting ridges in the final product somewhat resembling the stitches of sewing. While we were engaged in opposing the gas-welding patents, another suit was under way in Brooklyn based on those electric welding patents. We had no participation in that suit though I followed its course somewhat. Elyria won in the Brooklyn suit at about the time when it lost in our suit. Appeals were taken in both suits and the appeal in the electric welding suit came on for argument in the Court of Appeals in New York a few months after my return from the argument of our case before the Court of Appeals in Cincinnati. My interest in this whole subject led me to attend the argument of the electric welding suit in the Court of Appeals here. At the end of the argument, a large part of the audience got up and walked out of the courtroom and into an adjoining anteroom, among them myself and Myron Wick the President of Elyria. Wick and I happened to walk out together and as we emerged into the anteroom, he asked me what I thought about the argument and the prospect for a decision favorable to Elyria. He probably did not expect a very definite answer, or even a pertinent answer, but I had formed a definite opinion and thought I might as well let him have it. What I said to him was "I will answer your question this way. I will bet you $100 that you lose in Cincinnati, and another $100 that you win here." He was so flabbergasted at that reply that it took him some time to recover, and, when he did reply, he did not accept my proposition which I had occasion to regret later because, if he had accepted, he would have had to pay me $200.

All of this is preliminary to a much more important item. When we defeated the gas-welding patents in the Court of Appeals in Cincinnati, Elyria gave up on them. But there were various infringers of the electric welding patents, and Elyria wanted to prosecute them one after another, and in preparation for their next suit, Mr. Wick and a couple of his associates came around to see me and said that they wanted to retain our firm for the further litigation of their electric welding patents. From then on, there was active litigation of those patents, two suits in Brooklyn and one in New Jersey, in which we had many interesting experiences through a number of years up to the expiration of the electric welding patents.

There is another experience of the same kind in the firm's history which it is gratifying to recall. Back in the twenties, there was a company called Fibre Conduit Company[31] which made underfloor duct of a fibrous composition for use in wiring buildings for the installation of electrically-operated devices wherever it was desirable to have them by reason of the arrangement of the partitions and furniture in the space. Fibre Conduit thought it had a patent that dominated this business and brought suit and I took over the defense of the suit. While we were going through the preliminary stages of the litigation, someone thought it would be a smart idea to have the defendant, Walker Brothers, apply for a patent on its metallic form of this same duct, that it would be well for us to be able to say that defendant had filed an application for patent for its duct even if we had but little idea that a patent would ever be granted. So we put in an application. Eventually we got to trial over in Brooklyn, a trial wherein the principal items of interest were that the man who was to be the primary witness on our side suffered stage fright and loss of memory and was a complete flop, whereas another witness, one from whom we expected very little, stepped into the breach and performed nobly. Eventually we got a favorable decision (21 F.2d 756)[32] and the plaintiff appealed and we got an affirmance in the Court of Appeals (27 F.2d 708).[33] While these events were in progress, the application for patent on the steel duct became allowed and we issued a patent on it, and another company, National Electrical Products Company, of Pittsburgh, thought this under-floor duct business was attractive and entered upon the manufacture and sale of steel duct much like that offered by Walker Brothers. That, of course, made us take another look at the patent we had obtained for Walker Brothers, and, as we considered it further, we developed more and more respect for it. Ultimately our revised estimate of the patent got so high that we filed suit on it against National. Not only that, but we tried the suit and won it. Then National came around and asked for a license under the patent and that was worked out on appropriate terms. Then National came around again and told us they thought we had done so well in licking them that they wanted us to lick some others for them. From then on we had some years of active litigations in behalf of National, and, before very long after National was added to the fold, along came the representatives of Fibre Conduit and told us the same story, and thereupon we took on the patent work for Fibre Conduit Company and that has continued right down to the present day, though, in the meanwhile, the name of the company has been changed so that it is known to us at the present time as Orangeburg Manufacturing Company.

These instances are good illustrations of the potency of

success in professional controversies, in court and out of court, in enlarging the clientele of a law firm.

On this same subject, I strongly recommend active participation in associations of the bar, particularly the patent bar. It enlarges greatly one's friendships among members of the profession all over the country and one gets to know them personally as well as professionally. Also, it is quite common for professional employment to come from a personal friend who is practicing patent law in another city.

I have been a member of the New York Patent Law Association since its formation back in the early twenties, served as Vice-President two or three times and was President in 1941-42. Also, for many years I have been a member of the American Patent Law Association, the American Bar Association and the Association of the Bar of the City of New York.

In the American Bar Association I participated for many years in the activities of the Patent Section, attending many of the annual meetings at various cities around the country including Seattle, Chicago and St. Louis. This led to membership in the American Group of the International Association for the Protection of Industrial Property. Eventually I became President of the Group and served in that capacity for several years. My tenure of that office included the year 1947, and, in the summer of that year, I headed a small delegation which attended the biennial meeting of the International Association at The Hague, Holland. That was a very interesting experience, made the more interesting and pleasant by the association with John Dienner of Chicago and Dr. Stephen Ladas of New York who were members of the delegation.

Having obtained a client or a clientele, it is essential that he or they be served well and on that point it is well to remember that "the law is a jealous mistress." For the practice of patent law, one should have a good working knowledge of the fundamentals of physics, chemistry and mathematics so he can understand and fully assimilate all that is told to him by inventors and witnesses, including expert witnesses, both his own and his adversary's. Beyond that, he should know the law, the practice and the cases and know them fully and accurately and keep up to date on them constantly. That is a lifetime task. Any relaxation on it paves the way to a pitfall and a fall into the pit with consequent setback to the client's interest is wherein the jealousy of the mistress reveals itself. It may be guarded against adequately only by singleness of purpose and unremitting toil.

Maybe I did not learn this early enough. I think I came near qualifying as to unremitting toil, but not as to singleness of purpose. I did not devote myself exclusively to the law as my one and only mistress, but divided my effort between the law and business administration, including the management of investments, and some achievements back many years ago made me think I had some proficiency in that area. As the years went by, I assumed management functions in one company after another, and all of them interested me so much that, in the aggregate, I gave much time to them, time which might otherwise have been devoted to that jealous mistress I have mentioned by continuous probing into the principles and the evolution of the law and keeping abreast of changes, actual and impending, and the items pro and con bearing on them. The realization of this condition and recognition of the fact that I wanted to give more time and effort, rather than less to executive work as distinguished from professional work, led me some years ago to change my status in the firm to accord with the program I have since followed by giving less of my time and effort to the firm's professional work in order to make more time available for executive work for the several industrial and investment companies with which I have become associated.

Having said this much about practicing law and enlarging clientele, I might add a little more about housing the firm members who look after the clientele, supplementing the comment on 35 Nassau Street and the move to 165 Broadway.

Our quarters at 165 Broadway were very satisfactory indeed, and, over the years, we enlarged the space we had there, time after time, until ultimately we had the whole of the twenty-sixth floor of the building, and it was a very large floor. It was not unusual for people to suggest the installation of scooters for getting around the office, for if Mr. Morton at one end had occasion to see Mr. Mahoney at the other, he had to make a considerable allowance for "time in transit".

As a tenant at 165 Broadway, we had a succession of leases, mostly for five or three years. When a lease was about to expire, there was always talk about renewing or moving and after the first one or two such occurrences, the discussion was about whether to stay at 165 Broadway or move up to the Grand Central area.

When the lease was about to expire in 1940, this discussion went further than it ever had before, and, not unnaturally, most of the partners who lived in New Jersey did not take to the idea of moving uptown. Maybe I had quite a bit to do with the decision. The views presented in the discussion of this subject seemed to me to be rather evenly divided at a time when I had to go to Washington on an afternoon train, and, on the train, I wrote a letter addressed to Davis, in which I said that, after much reflection over this matter, I thought it would be best for the firm to move uptown and definitely favored that program. When I got back from my Washington trip, there seemed to be complete accord that we should move uptown if we could find suitable quarters.

## Enlarging Clientele

In the years prior to that, I had on various occasions gone into 247 Park Avenue on the seventeenth and eighteenth floors at the office of the Bakelite Company; I had a number of patent matters with Bakelite in which I represented Flintkote. Growing out of that association with the Bakelite attorney, I learned that the Bakelite Company had been acquired by Union Carbide, that Union had moved the whole Bakelite organization out of 247 Park Avenue and over into its main office on 42nd Street, and that the Bakelite lease on the two floors in 247 Park Avenue had two more years to run at a rental of $20,000 a year with no prospect of being able to sublet for the unexpired term of the lease. I told some of the partners about this and they seemed to think well of taking on those seventeenth and eighteenth floors as our new office.

At that point I called my friend George Baekeland, son of the Bakelite inventor, on the telephone at his office in Union Carbide and arranged to see him that morning. Immediately after passing the time of day with him, I said, "George, I came here to offer to give you $20,000." That startled him a bit and he demanded an explanation, and, after restating the salient facts about the unexpired lease at 247 Park Avenue, I told him I had come there to offer him $20,000 for his lease. He said it was interesting but that he would have to confer with the real estate people of his company and would let me have an answer very soon, probably the next day. With that I went back to 165 Broadway, and, within minutes after I got there, I was called on the telephone by George Baekeland who told me my offer was accepted. All of the partners seemed to welcome the news, both the moving to 247 Park Avenue and the saving of $20,000, and, in our innocence, we figured that this $20,000 saved would cover the cost of rearranging and redecorating the new office to fit our needs. This refurbishing job actually cost more than two and a half times that amount, but, even so, we lived for a while in the thought that we would take over our new quarters at no expense beyond what we had saved on the lease.

The move uptown was made with some reservations on the part of a few of the partners, but, before we had been at the uptown location very long, everyone seemed to be enthusiastic about it, and, of course, those who welcomed the move most were the ones who, like myself, lived out in Westchester or Connecticut during a part or all of the year. Even the ones who lived in New Jersey found but little difficulty in travel to our new location. A census we conducted over a period of a month indicated that four out of five clients coming to see us at our office found it more convenient to see us at our uptown location rather than at a Wall Street address, and, when we went out of our office on business errands, it was four times out of five that starting from our uptown location rather than the downtown one was more convenient. That census was back in 1940 when conditions were quite different from what they are today. If anyone in the firm were now to put forward the view that we should move back to a Wall Street location, I think he would not even get a respectful hearing.

# Dry Kilns for Treating Lumber

In the late twenties, Mr. Sage and I had some unusual experiences in two litigations relating to kilns for treating lumber. No great principle of patent law was involved, no considerable amount of money was at stake, and the attorney representing the opposition was not very formidable. But there were occurrences in the courtrooms where the two cases were tried which were unusual and entertaining, and I have said occasionally that one of those two suits ranks as the high point of professional achievement in all of my experiences at the Bar.

There was a young man by the name of Welch who was a classmate of Mr. Sage at M.I.T. The intimacy which developed there continued through later years in which Sage became a partner of our firm and Welch became the President and executive officer of Welch Dry Kiln Company, specializing in making and installing kilns for drying lumber. Welch thought he had made an invention in that art and Sage got him a patent for it. Later it appeared that there were various infringers down in the south and we had to undertake to suppress them.

First, there was a suit that came on for trial down in New

Orleans and Sage and I went down there and tried it. The principal witness on our side had to be Welch and he was a curious problem, nervous and fidgety, very active mentally and physically but lacking the guidance of good judgment. In this New Orleans case, he was at his worst. As a witness he sat at a table which was an extension of the Judge's bench and he kept trying to reach across the table and make signals to Sage and myself indicating what he thought we should do, assuming, quite without justification, that His Honor could not see what he was doing and ignoring completely the simple fact that even if the Judge could not see him, the opposing attorney could. We did what we could to make him leave to us the matters other than testifying, but without making much progress. His Honor displayed great patience, more than most Judges would have. Finally the Judge concluded that some interposition by him would not be amiss, and that led him to comment, as accurately as I can recall it, as follows: "It may be that if we continue with what we have been doing, we will demonstrate the truth of the ancient maxim that a man who is his own attorney has a fool for a client."

Notwithstanding Welch's performance, we got the decree we sought (26 Fed. 2d, 810)[34] and an affirmance on appeal (39 Fed. 2d, 589).[35]

Shortly after that, a suit against an infringer in Mississippi based on the Welch patent came on for trial and we all assembled at Biloxi, Mississippi, an attractive little town on the coast of the Gulf of Mexico midway between New Orleans and Mobile. The case came on before District Judge E.R. Holmes who had never tried a patent case, and, so far as we ascertained, had never had occasion to know about a patent. He had not been on the bench long and in his experience up to that date his judicial work had been concerned almost entirely with negroes

**Plate i.** Dean Stockett Edmonds, ca. 1940

**Plate ii.** John C. Pennie, ca. 1914

**Plate iii.** The youthful Mr. and Mrs. John C. and Alida York Pennie, ca. 1885

**Plate iv.** Dean Edmonds at the 1937 Christmas party in the firm's offices at 165 Broadway in New York City

**Plate v.** Frank E. Barrows, ca. 1950

**Plate vi.** The legal staff of Pennie, Davis, Marvin & Edmonds on the occasion of the 1933 annual firm dinner at the University Club in New York City. Dean Edmonds is shown seated at the table, seventh from the left.

**Plate vii.**
The legal staff of Pennie, Edmonds, Morton, Barrows & Taylor at the firm's May 19, 1955 annual dinner at the University Club. **Shown standing, beginning from the left:** W. Brown Morton Jr., Andrew K. McColpin, Clyde C. Metzger, Helmer W. Anderson, Adam V. Hohmuth (accounting), David Weild, Jr., James W. Laist, Robert McKay, Robert B. Buckley, Baldwin Guild, Frank E. Barrows, R. Morton Adams, W. Brown Morton, Raymond B. Canfield, Clarence M. Fisher, George W. Cooper, Leslie B. Young, Noel G. Conway, John C. Dorfman, Frank F. Scheck, J. Philip Anderegg, Arnold R. Workman, Merton W. Sage, and Harry C. Olson (accounting). **Shown seated, beginning from the left:** Eugene C. Buck, S. Leslie Misrock, S. Howell Brown Jr., Harry R. Sage, Merton S. Neill, Hubert G. Moore, Jr., Daniel V. Mahoney, Hubert T. Mandeville, Dean S. Edmonds, John T. Farley, Harold A. Traver, George R. Douglas, George E. Middleton, Thomas F. Reddy, Jr., Stanton T. Lawrence, Jr., Edward B. Hunter, George Larounis, Willis H. Taylor, Jr., and Vergil L. Gerard.

**Plate viii.**
The legal staff of Pennie Edmonds, Morton, Taylor & Adams at the 1968 annual firm dinner at the University Club. **Shown Standing, beginning from the left:** *Charles E. McKenney, Joseph J.C. Ranalli, Adam V. Hohmuth (foreign accounting), Harry C. Olson (accounting), Shui-Tong Hui, Arnold R. Workman, Lewis S. Reff, John H. Shaida (accounting), Edward J. Gorman, Jr., Vernon L. Ringler, William A. Victor, James G. Foley, William E. Hanford, Jr., William E. Ringle, James F. Bryan, Philip T. Shannon, Harry C. Jones, III, John T. Ronan, III, James D. Donohoe, Frank Cieffo, (unidentified), Jonathan A. Marshall, Jeffrey A. Rosen, John L. Downing, Harold A. Traver, (unidentified), Bert W. Leonardson (office manager), Ambrose A. Arnold, and Berj A. Terzian.* **Shown seated, beginning from the left:** *David Weild, III, Harry R. Sage, Merton S. Neill, Hubert G. Moore, Jr., Raymond B. Canfield, Frank F. Scheck, Leslie B. Young, Dean S. Edmonds, Thomas F. Reddy, Jr., Willis H. Taylor, Jr., R. Morton Adams, W. Philip Anderegg, S. Leslie Misrock, Robert J. Kadel, Clyde C. Metzger, and David J. Toomey.*

**Plate ix.**
Partners of Pennie & Edmonds at the firm's annual dinner, Pierre Hotel, New York City, 1996.

**Shown standing, back row, beginning from the left:** *Allan A. Fanucci, Jonathan E. Moskin, Bruce J. Barker, Jon R. Stark, Gidon D. Stern, Isaac Jarkovsky, Barry D. Rein, David Weild, III, John M. Richardson, Philip T. Shannon, Charles E. Miller, Samuel B. Abrams, James N. Palik, Peter D. Vogl, Gerald J. Flintoft, Marcia H. Sundeen, and Joseph Diamante.*

**Shown standing, middle row, beginning from the left:** *James W. Dabney, Stephen J. Harbulak, Albert P. Halluin, Donald J. Goodell, Charles E. McKenney, Brian M. Poissant, John J. Lauter, Jr., John J. Normile, Stanton T. Lawrence, III, and Adriane M. Antler.*
**Shown seated, beginning from the left:** *Laura A. Coruzzi, Francis E. Morris, Brian D. Coggio, Berj A. Terzian, S. Leslie Misrock, Victor N. Balancia, Harry C. Jones, III, Rory J. Radding, and Geraldine F. Baldwin.*

on the one hand and district attorneys on the other and with issues arising under the prohibition laws.

Again Mr. Welch was present and again it was necessary for him to be the principal witness for plaintiff. He was in a state of agitation greater than ever before. He knew he was going to be in a state of agitation and so he brought his wife to the courtroom to sit beside him there. We opened with the usual statements of counsel as to what the case was all about. After these statements had been concluded, I got up and was about to call plaintiff's first witness when the Judge seemed to indicate that he wanted to say something. We stopped and waited and we were kept waiting for an extended period during which the Judge seemed to be struggling with some problem incident to expressing what he had on his mind. Finally out it came. He looked down at me and said, "Would you please tell me what it is that a Judge decides in a case like this?"

We did the best we could with our explanations and then got started with testimony which ran on through the whole of the day. The next day we assembled and again Welch knew that he was going to need moral support beside him and on this second day he brought his mother with him to the courtroom. Again we went on through the day with testimony, and, as on the first day, the Judge said little on any subject and nothing bordering in any way upon patents or patent law.

We got fairly close to the finish on the second day but had to run over into the third day, and, when we assembled in the courtroom on that third day, Mr. Welch had both his wife and mother beside him. Before the end of the morning, we came to the finish of the trial. My adversary and I informed the Court that we rested and waited for him to give some indication as to what program he wanted to follow. There was a long wait but His Honor said nothing. Finally, because something had to be done to break the silence, I inquired whether His Honor wanted us to present our arguments at once or would prefer that we prepare and file briefs and have the oral argument at a later date. Again there was a long silence in which the Judge seemed to be wrestling with some abstruse problem. Again there was nothing for us to do but wait and that is what we did. After a long silence, the Judge finally broke in with a crisp short statement "I think I am ready to decide this case right now." We all sat down in more or less of a semicircle across the courtroom with His Honor seated in a lonely state up on a high bench, and obviously the only thing to do was to sit there and wait until His Honor elected to proceed. Again we waited through a long period of silence. We assumed that the Judge was formulating his views for oral presentation, but there was nothing we could do about that, so we sat there and waited. Finally the Judge erupted with a single short statement, "The Court decides the case in favor of the plaintiff." That was all there was to it.

But what came immediately after that is what I have been trying to get to. Mr. Welch was rendered speechless by the Court's announcement, but before long he came to realize that his side of the case had won and that meant to him that he must be up and doing something. With nothing better to do, he strode across the front of the courtroom, over to me, and grabbed me by the hand, and pump-handled my arm with great vigor. That was all well enough, but along with it came something more. Welch's wife followed him across the courtroom in my direction, and, while he was pump-handling my arm, she kissed me. That, I submit as the high point of my professional career. So far as I know, there are few patent attorneys who can claim that they have attained that high pinnacle of fame.

I might add that the case was appealed and was affirmed on

appeal (33 F.(2d) 117).[36] I might add also that Judge Holmes learned how to be a Federal Judge very quickly and very well and before many years after our appearance before him, he was made a Judge of the Circuit Court of Appeals for the Fifth Circuit and served in that capacity for many years during which there were many tributes to his ability.

# Rubber Accelerators

THE LITIGATION OF A PATENT FOR A RUBBER ACCELERATOR WAS interesting because of the checkered course it followed in which we suffered two severe setbacks and because it ended in the Supreme Court where we obtained complete vindication. Also, the opinion of the Supreme Court has become the authority on the proposition that a claim for a class of substances should be held invalid if there are members of the class which are not usable in the practice of the patented invention.

Back in the twenties, the rubber manufacturing industry began to use in a large way certain chemicals known as accelerators for expediting the process of vulcanization. For a time, the preferred accelerator was a substance known as diphenylguanidine, and Dovan Chemical Company obtained a patent for the use of that chemical as an accelerator. Dovan brought suit against National Aniline & Chemical Company, later a constituent of Allied Chemical,[37] and Mr. Barrows and I took on the defense of the suit. We tried it in the District Court in New York before Circuit Judge Martin T. Manton, and we tried the case very well. Even so, Judge Manton held the patent valid and infringed. We took an appeal, and, at the argument of the appeal, everything went our way, with the result that the adverse decision below was reversed, the Appellate Court holding the patent invalid (292 Fed. 555).[38]

The owner of the patent was unwilling to quit at that point and brought a suit against another alleged infringer in another Circuit. It brought the suit in Pittsburgh against a rubber manufacturer by the name of Corona Cord Tire Company which bought its diphenylguanidine from duPont and duPont asked us to take over the defense. We had a most interesting trial before Judge Gibson at Pittsburgh. In this trial, for the first time in my experience, I made use of a handwriting expert. A date in a laboratory record book became a critical date and I had a handwriting expert examine the date in the original record book and report his findings, not telling him anything about how the date fitted into the situation. After this handwriting expert had made his examination at an uptown office where the original record was made available, he reported to me in very positive terms that the entry in the laboratory record book had been changed and he stated equally positively what the date recorded had been before it was changed. Because he could state on the witness stand that his report was made with no knowledge of what the conflicting contentions were, I decided to put him on the witness stand as part of a vigorous attack upon the veracity of the patentee of the patent in suit.

Judge Gibson decided the case in our favor, and, in doing so, he held specifically that the patentee of the patent in suit who had testified at length at the trial was unworthy of belief (10 F. 2d, 598).[39]

The patent owner took an appeal, and, for the argument on appeal, it retained the services of the Honorable John W. Davis who had returned to the practice of law after an unsuccessful campaign for election to the Presidency. Mr. Davis's mellifluous argument before the Court of Appeals, and possibly also some deficiencies on my part, resulted in a reversal of the District Court's ruling (16 F.2d, 419).[40]

So we had conflicting decisions of two Courts of Appeals, following upon conflicting decisions of two District Courts. Certiorari was plainly in order, so we applied for the writ and it was granted. We had a most interesting argument before the Supreme Court, presided over by Chief Justice Taft. I had a great advantage over my adversary in that I had been in the case throughout the proceedings in the trial courts and he had not. In the course of his argument, Mr. Davis made a definite statement of fact which he would not have made had he been more familiar with the record, and, in my reply argument, it was possible to contradict him flatly with a pat reference to the record. The point involved was not one of great importance, but the way it developed in the courtroom made it assume an importance well beyond what it deserved. The result was that the Supreme Court reversed the Court of Appeals, with a unanimous opinion written by the Chief Justice, and so, after suffering the two defeats in the lower courts, we obtained complete vindication (276 U.S. 358).[41]

Although the Supreme Court held the patent in suit invalid, it did not sustain the finding of District Judge Gibson that the patentee of the patent in suit was unworthy of belief. On receipt of the opinion, I wrote to Judge Gibson telling him about it and I took occasion to add in my letter that while we welcomed the Supreme Court's conclusion of invalidity, I was strongly of the opinion that of the seventeen Judges who had had occasion to pass on that accelerator patent, he was the only one who had decided the case as I thought it should be decided, namely, that the patentee of the patent in suit, the critical witness for the plaintiff, had testified falsely and had altered an original record.

This series of five court proceedings extending over a period of years was started by the adverse decision of Judge Manton in the New York District Court, and it developed later that this Judge Manton, a member of the Court of Appeals bench, was a man of low moral fibre who would even stoop to the low level of shaping his court decisions in response to financial remuneration. We never had any reason for thinking that Judge Manton was influenced improperly in his decision in the accelerator case. But, some years later, he gave us a shock which caused us to speculate on his integrity. Mr. Mahoney and I took on the defense of a suit on a patent for a heat-treating furnace. We tried it before Judge Woolsey in the District Court in New York City, and we had some sound defenses and presented them very convincingly. Judge Woolsey sustained all of our contentions with an opinion which we thought was beyond attack (18 F. Supp. 871).[42] The defendant took an appeal and the argument in the Court of Appeals came on before Judges Manton, Learned Hand and Swan. The argument in the Court of Appeals went very well and left us with no doubt of an affirmance. To our utter amazement, the Court of Appeals reversed, with a colorless opinion by Manton, concurred in by Swan, and a short, crisp dissenting opinion by Learned Hand (96 F. 2d, 61).[43] The condition presented was so amazing that I talked with Judge Hand about it in his chambers. He was as nonplussed as I; I got a strong feeling that he was much troubled in his mind about the condition presented but felt he had to restrain himself from speaking his mind fully. Even then, none of us suspected that Judge Manton's decision could be bought. We did know that a strong hostility had developed between Judge Manton and Judge Woolsey, growing out of decisions in controversies affecting the New York subways, and so we were inclined to ascribe this reversal by the Court of Appeals, with Judge Learned Hand dissenting, to Manton's willingness to disregard the merits of our case in order to strike back at Judge Woolsey.

It was not long after that litigation that the truth began to come out about Judge Manton. The F.B.I. conducted a thorough investigation of payments received, income tax returns, etc., and soon Manton was indicted. After a long trial, he was found guilty and served a jail sentence, one of the few Federal Judges to suffer that form of disgrace.

Having recorded that much about Judge Manton, I might add something further. Some intimacy developed between us by reason of the numerous cases I had before him, and, on one or two occasions when he was to speak before a patent group, he sought my aid in deciding on what to say and how to say it. Then on one occasion when I was with him, he told me he was thinking of resigning from the bench and returning to the practice of law. He named a couple of prominent law firms which he thought would be glad to welcome him, and then went on to say that he had had so much experience in patent cases while on the bench that he thought he would be quite an asset to an established firm of patent practitioners, and he went on to suggest that maybe we would like to take him into our firm as an eminent counsel heading the firm. That put me in a sad predicament; I knew we did not want Manton with us and yet how could I tell him so without the danger of some repercussion in a litigation which came before him? At our next meeting, I told him it was not possible for us to take him into our firm, and, among other things, I mentioned that one reason for this was that we had recently taken in Mr. A.G. Davis who had retired as a Vice-President of the General Electric Company. Fortunately, I got by that part of what I had to say very well. Then I went on to mention other patent firms which might well be considered, particularly the firm of Hoguet & Neary, because that firm had grown very fast over the years up to that time, and both Hoguet and Neary were Catholic, as Judge Manton was. That resulted in various meetings between Hoguet and Neary and Manton, and, for a while, their talks seemed to be progressing toward a partnership of the three of them. Fortunately for our good friends Hoguet and Neary, something happened to prevent that proposal from being consummated.

Having brought Hoguet & Neary into this narrative, I might add that I was responsible for the formation of that firm. My good friend, Ramsay Hoguet, after some years of service in one or more of the large patent law firms, started in practice for himself and prospered considerably. His clientele grew in number and importance to the point where he could not fulfill all their demands, and his assistants, while capable up to a point, were unable to take over in a way that satisfied the clients who sought Hoguet's services. Hoguet told me about this condition, saying that he needed to have with him someone of mature judgment and extended experience. We canvassed the members of the patent bar in our quest for likely candidates and I arranged for Hoguet to meet one or two whom I thought were promising. Then, it occurred to me that Jack Neary fulfilled all of the requirements we had in mind. He had grown up in Wilmington and practiced law there for years and had much experience in patent matters in the Delaware Court in cases where he represented out-of-town counsel. Neary had moved to New York and was practicing law here, but, because he was not well known here, his clientele was not of a size commensurate with his ability. The more I thought of Jack Neary, the more it seemed to me that he had all of the qualifications we had in mind for a partnership with Ramsay Hoguet, so I arranged for these two men to meet me for lunch at the Bankers Club. The meeting was followed by two or three other meetings and all developed quite favorably. The one time I asked them to lunch with me again at the Bankers Club at one o'clock on that day, I phoned the Bankers Club and told them that I had invited two guests there to lunch with me and found I could not get there for lunch and I wanted these two men to be given that message and to be told that they were to have lunch together and sign my name to the luncheon check. The scheme worked like a charm. They made progress toward a partnership far more rapidly than they would have had I been present. And, shortly thereafter, I was told that they had come to a complete agreement. Before long they leased a rather considerable office down in Broad Street and they proceeded to furnish it elaborately and very attractively. Then one time they called me on the phone and said I had to have lunch with them and at lunch they told me that was the first day of the new firm and after lunch I would have to go with them and inspect their new office. I did that and complimented them appropriately on their new quarters. On my return to my office, there was a large package on my desk addressed to me, and, on opening it, I found a set of four large and very fine old English Sporting prints. Along with this attractive present was a brief note signed by Hoguet and Neary and stating that the set of prints was "my fee for acting as the marriage broker." These fine prints now hang in my home at Fairfield, Connecticut, and are highly prized both for what they are and for how I got them.

 The new firm prospered and some years later was joined by Worthington Campbell and became Hoguet, Neary & Campbell. Still later it was joined by Granville Brumbaugh and then later by Walter Free who had been with us for some years as my assistant. Both Ramsay Hoguet and Jack Neary died prematurely but the firm which they established has carried on in a big way and is now known widely and favorably under the name Brumbaugh, Free, Graves and Donohue.

# Pelletted Carbon Black

This is another litigation which followed a course like that of the rubber accelerator patent in the respect that we had to take a couple of lickings. Also, the case went to the Supreme Court and it ended with complete success for our side and large recovery for our client, Columbian Carbon Company.[44]

Back in Mr. Pennie's day, we did patent work from time to time for Binney & Smith, a prosperous sales agency for chemical products. I think Mr. Binney and Mr. Smith were personal friends of Mr. Pennie and they were men of fine character and great business ability. Among other products sold by Binney & Smith was carbon black, which, in those early years, was used primarily in ink, crayons and products of that sort. Later it was found that carbon black was outstandingly useful as a reinforcing agent in articles made of vulcanized rubber, particularly automobile tires. It was a better reinforcing agent than zinc oxide which had been used, and in the course of a few years the use of zinc oxide was superseded by carbon black almost entirely.

Binney & Smith had been the sales agents for a number of small companies producing carbon black and along in the twenties they were instrumental in putting those carbon black companies together under the name Columbian Carbon Company. Columbian prospered right from the start, the volume of carbon black used in making automobile tires increased enormously, and Columbian continued through the years to be one of the largest of the suppliers of carbon black. Also it has always been and now is a client of our firm.

Somewhere in the organizations of Binney & Smith and Columbian Carbon, a valuable improvement was made in producing carbon black in the form of small round pellets or aggregates, whereby important advantages were obtained, particularly in handling the carbon black both in the plants where it was made and in the rubber plants where it was used.

We took out a patent covering this invention, both the product itself and the process of making it. The invention was put into use in a big way by Columbian, and, after the lapse of but a few years, other manufacturers of carbon black became envious and one of them, United Carbon Company, could not resist the temptation to copy what Columbian had done.

We filed suit in the name of Binney & Smith Company against United Carbon Company down in Charleston, West Virginia, and the suit came on for trial there before Judge Barksdale of Virginia who was substituting for some West Virginia Judge. We presented our case very well indeed, being aided considerably by our adversary who put on the stand a man who gave some exceedingly unimportant testimony for the defendant, and, on cross-examination, some invaluable testimony for plaintiff. Even so, Judge Barksdale decided against us. (37 F. Supp. 779)[45]

We appealed to the Court of Appeals for the Fourth Circuit and there all was different. Not only did we get a reversal (125 F. 2d, 255),[46] but the opinion rendered by presiding Judge

Parker was all that the most hopeful advocate could ask — we could not have done better if he had asked us to write it.

The defeated defendant petitioned the Supreme Court for certiorari. There seemed to be no reason whatever why the Supreme Court should grant certiorari, but it did. In the course of time we got before the Supreme Court for argument, with ex-Judge Morris of Wilmington, Delaware, representing United Carbon, and, to all outward appearances, it seemed that in the argument we had come out on top by a wide margin, the more so because Judge Morris spent much of his time reading from his draft of what he thought he wanted to say, with the resultant loss of interest on the part of the Justices. However, the decision of the Supreme Court was against us (317 U.S. 228).[47] The Court's opinion included much comment that was disconcerting but what it actually held was that the two claims in suit were vague and indefinite, too much so to permit of sustaining them. That was a bitter blow to us, coming as it did after an opinion by the Court of Appeals which was so wonderful, and after an argument which we had thought was so favorable.

For a while, we were bogged down in despair. Before long, however, we recovered, and, in the process of recovery, we evolved the idea of reissuing the patent with the two claims sued upon amended to include words of definition at the points where the Supreme Court said they were indefinite.[48] The application for reissue was filed and we had a rough time getting it through the Patent Office. The Primary Examiner realized that if he reissued the patent, the reissue would be submitted for review by a Court and therefore he had better not stick his neck out. Nothing could budge him, even in personal interviews where his every argument was obliterated. So we appealed to the Board.[49] The same condition seemed to affect the members of the Board and there we got another rebuff.

Then we went to Commissioner Coe and pressed upon him with great vigor our contention that we were entitled to reissue. The Commissioner finally said he would treat our application to him as an application for a rehearing before the Examiners-in-Chief and he arranged to have the rehearing granted. So we had the rehearing before the Examiners-in-Chief and I put forward a most strenuous effort in presenting my view to the Board. In the finale of the argument, there was an element of the dramatic in it. Fortunately it worked. The effort was successful and the reissue was granted.

We made preparations for filing another suit against the same defendant, United Carbon Company, even in advance of the reissuance of the patent. United found out about the reissue in some way[50] and prepared to file suit immediately on its issuance for a declaratory judgement[51] of invalidity and both parties chose Baltimore as the place of the trial. It so happened that the United Carbon suit got filed first; it was filed on a Friday, I think the Friday following the Tuesday when the patent was issued, whereas our suit did not get filed until the following Monday because our Baltimore representative went on a fishing trip over the weekend.

Shortly after that, we got before Judge Coleman in the District Court at Baltimore on some preliminary matters, and, when they were disposed of, I proposed that the two suits be combined, that each complaint be considered an answer to the other complaint, and that the case be declared to be at issue[52] forthwith. That seemed to appeal to Judge Coleman and an appropriate order was entered to that effect. Then I pointed out to the Judge that, with the case thus at issue, it would seem to be appropriate to set it down for trial, whereupon he asked me when I wanted to try it, and I answered, "Tomorrow or next week, or next month." At that, Judge Coleman looked down at me with amazement and finally said, "Well, you are a novelty." I did not know the Judge then as well as I got to know him later, so I was at somewhat of a loss to know what reply to make, with the result that there was a long silence during which the Judge continued to look down at me. Finally he broke the silence by saying, "You are the first patent attorney I have ever known who wanted to try his case right away."

We did get to trial within a few months and the trial was a continuous grand experience so far as we were concerned, and exceedingly disconcerting for our adversary. The adversary continued to be represented by ex-Judge Morris and Morris had evolved a theory which he thought was overwhelming. It was an unsound theory and Judge Coleman was fully satisfied that it was unsound long before Morris stopped expounding it.

Then the defense put on the witness stand an eminent scientist from the University of Michigan. He may have been quite a scholar in his chosen branch of science, but his training in courtroom conduct and comment had been woefully neglected. His worst mistake was to refer to the opinion of the Court of Appeals in the prior suit as "silly". He could not have said anything that would have prejudiced him more with Judge Colemen. When we reassembled on the morning after this comment occurred, I think everyone from Judge Coleman down to the bailiff noted that this eminent scientist was not among those present and defendant's counsel never referred to him again.

We came to the end of the trial in three or four days and Judge Coleman announced his opinion in our favor orally at the close of the trial. Following his practice, he would not allow any of us to have a stenographic transcript of his remarks, but a few weeks later he filed an edited copy of his remarks as his opinion (59 F. Supp. 384).[53]

At this point in the litigation, the defendant was in a sad

plight. The only right of appeal it had was an appeal to the Court of Appeals which had already held the patent in suit valid with an opinion lauding the patented invention as an achievement of high order and the patent as one whose validity should be considered beyond question. The prospect did not appear at all alluring to the defendant, and, when other producers of carbon black in pelletized form came to a realization of the conditions presented, they were much disturbed as to what was going to happen to them. That resulted in a series of meetings of officers of the several companies, and, following one of these meetings, a representative of United Carbon came to me and told me about the meetings and said that he was authorized to say that all of the infringers in the industry would become licensees and pay royalty to Columbian if the royalty rate were what they thought of as reasonable. They told me of the royalty rate they were willing to pay, and, on referring this to Columbian Carbon, that rate was accepted. Following quickly after that, all of the manufacturers in the industry became licensees and they paid royalty quarterly up to the expiration of the patent. So Columbian got complete vindication, and, over the remaining five years of the term of the reissued patent, it collected about a hundred thousand dollars a year in royalties.

# United States Supreme Court

I have referred in the foregoing to four of our patent litigations which went to the Supreme Court; the pelleted carbon black case, the rubber accelerator case, the welding torch case which produced the famous Davis-Bournonville decision, and the artificial lard case. I had but little participation in the artificial lard case, almost nothing beyond my talks with Mr. Barrows to which I have referred and sitting in the courtrooms when Mr. Pennie tried the case and argued the appeal. In the other three cases, I presented the argument in the Supreme Court. I was well satisfied with my presentation in the rubber accelerator and carbon black cases, but far from satisfied with my presentation in the Davis-Bournonville case, though I might add that I think neither Daniel Webster nor Joseph Choate could have presented an argument for the plaintiff in that case which would have prevailed.

It is distinctly unusual for a patent litigation to get into the Supreme Court. One could practice patent law in the United States quite actively for forty years and never have occasion to appear in the Supreme Court. We, in our firm, have been a pronounced exception to the general rule in that area, for there have been many times when we have appeared there.

The first case in which I appeared in the Supreme Court was in a suit in the United States Court of Claims[54] in behalf of Electric Boat Company, now a constituent of General Dynamics Company. Mr. Davis started that suit, but when he left us to take up war work in World War I on supply contracts under General Goethals, I took over, and, after Davis's return, I had gotten way along with it and his absorption in other matters prevented him from taking it over.

A great deal of testimony was taken by deposition and that was followed by briefs and an argument before the Court of Claims. Some months later the Court filed an opinion presenting the several issues quite fully and discussing them intelligently and judicially and upholding our contentions on all of them.

Before anything further could be done, the Department of Justice obtained new counsel including Frederick Emery who headed a Boston firm and Edgar Bull of Gifford & Bull here in New York, and these new counsel presented a motion for reopening for the purpose of introducing newly discovered evidence. Under well established rules, this motion should have been denied, but it was granted and the new counsel introduced a considerable amount of additional testimony, none of it involving anything newly discovered or anything that was at all persuasive. Then we had another argument before the Court in which the new counsel for the Government made only passing reference to the testimony taken on the reopening. They reargued the whole case with little reference to that evidence. After the lapse of several months, the Court filed an opinion of a couple of dozen lines, containing no intelligent discussion whatever but reversing its former decision (57 Ct. Cls. 497-514).[55]

We appealed the case to the Supreme Court and Mr. Fish

and I presented the argument there, but it was to no avail. The Supreme Court affirmed with an opinion by Associate Justice Oliver Wendall Holmes (263 U.S. 621).[56]

If ever an applicant for justice in a Court got a raw deal it was in that case in the Court of Claims. The Court reversed itself with no statement of why it receded from the conclusions it had stated so fully and clearly in its previous decision and without any reference to the testimony taken on the reopening for further testimony for which there was no justification.

We were told by a member of the staff of the office of the Clerk of the Court of Claims that the Judges who heard the case on the second argument fought over it in conference with great vigor time and again, and that, toward the end of one of the conferences, one of the Judges walked out of the conference room in high dudgeon and slammed the door behind him with some strident remarks disclosing great irritability. However, all we got was that second so-called opinion, very short and utterly meaningless except for the statement that the Court had reversed itself.

One of the difficulties in that case was that our claim was for a large sum, that is, what was considered a large amount in those days, not now. It could not have been otherwise in accordance with the basis for our claim. There was one change in the personnel of the Bench of the Court of Claims in the interval between the two arguments in our case and we were told that the new member of the Bench was the one who carried the Court over to the reversal. He seemed to feel that he and his brethren had to function as "watchdogs of the Treasury" rather than as ministers of justice, or maybe he was fearful of criticism of the Court of Claims, himself included, in and out of Congress, if the Court authorized a large award.

Another case of ours which went to the Supreme Court was the ethylene oxide case in which we represented U.S. Industrial

Chemicals, then controlled by Air Reduction.[57] It was a suit for infringement of a reissued patent. Mr. Barrows and I tried that case down in Baltimore before Judge Coleman, but nothing we presented seemed to make an impression on him and he sustained the patent (34 Fed. Supp. 813).[58]

We took an appeal and thought we presented a winning argument, but the Court of Appeals thought otherwise (121 F. 2d. 665).[59] We decided to apply for <u>certiorari</u>, and, in connection with that petition, Davis came into the case with us. Fortunately for us, our petition impressed the Supreme Court favorably and the petition was granted. We put great effort into our brief in the Supreme Court; Davis became very much interested and worked hard and well on the brief. Also, he presented the argument in the Supreme Court. What is even more important, the argument prevailed. The Supreme Court reversed the decisions below on the sound ground that the reissued patent was not a patent for the invention for which the original patent was granted (315 U.S. 668).[60]

The patent owner was not satisfied to quit at that point. It obtained a second reissue, directed to curing what the Supreme Court had found to be a defect in the first reissue. Then we had a merry time over a jurisdictional issue. Immediately on the issuance of the second reissue, we filed a suit here in New York for a declaratory judgement that the second reissue was invalid. Within a short time thereafter, plaintiff filed a suit against us down in Baltimore for infringement of this second reissue. Then the patent owner moved to dismiss our New York suit and we moved to dismiss the Baltimore suit. We defeated defendant's motion here and also we got our motion in Baltimore sustained, whereupon the adversary appealed the Baltimore case but appealed unsuccessfully.

The argument of the appeal on this jurisdictional issue in

the Baltimore case was one out of which I got great satisfaction because there was much discussion between the members of the Bench and myself about why it was that the Supreme Court reversed both the Court of Appeals and the District Court, and why it was that we preferred to litigate the issue presented in the New York Courts rather than in Baltimore. Among other things I told the Court that in the Supreme Court the opposition, then represented by new counsel, the redoubtable Sam Darby, had thrown overboard the decision of the Court of Appeals and presented a new theory in support of its claim and that the Supreme Court's opinion discussed both the old theory and the new one and overruled both of them, and I added that I would not attempt to explain why plaintiff's counsel abandoned the decision of the Court of Appeals in the Supreme Court, but, instead, would leave that to my adversary.

After this jurisdictional issue was disposed of in both Circuits much to our satisfaction, we prepared for trial and the case came on before Judge Coxe here in New York with Mr. Barrows and myself representing the opposition to the patent. Before Judge Coxe, everything went as well for us as it had gone badly before Judge Coleman down in Baltimore. Judge Coxe sustained a number of our defense propositions (67 Fed. Supp. 895),[61] and sustaining any one of them would have sufficed. It must be that the patent owner was quite overwhelmed at that point because it did not take an appeal.

Another important litigation of ours which went to the Supreme Court involved the modern washing machines of the motor-driven-agitator type.

Back in the early thirties, The Maytag Company brought suit for infringement of a formidable looking washing machine patent against Brooklyn Edison Company which had sold some machines of a well-known make, and we took over the defense of the suit in behalf of the manufacturer.

The case came on for trial before Judge Byers in the Brooklyn Court and the trial extended over many days, with much time devoted to demonstrations in the courtroom. The Judge came down on the floor of the courtroom and sat beside the machines as they were operated and seemed to assimilate all we were trying to demonstrate, and he made copious notes day after day. We thought we tried the case very well. Unfortunately for us, the testimony and demonstrations which we thought were so convincing did not seem to register with Judge Byers and he filed an opinion characterized by much length, and, we thought, little sense. The gist of it, following a long rambling discourse, was that he was left with the "impression" that the plaintiff had "done something". He did not go on to say what it was that he was left with the impression the plaintiff had done, or whether the patent in suit disclosed whatever it was that he was left with the impression the plaintiff had done, or whether the patent contained a claim for whatever it was that he was left with the impression the plaintiff had done. He seemed to think that since the trial was a long one, the opinion should be a long one, so he put into his opinion great length and little else except that at the end he held the patent in suit valid and infringed. (11 F. Supp. 743)[62]

We took an appeal and Davis got so much interested in the case in the course of the preparation of the appeal brief that he took over the argument in the Court of Appeals. All three Judges of the Court of Appeals assimilated everything he presented and seemed to be ready to hold the patent in suit invalid at the end of the argument. Defendant's counsel, Wallace R. Lane of Chicago, whom I have mentioned heretofore, faced a pretty tough situation right from the start of his argument.

Probing questions from the members of the Bench disconcerted him more and more, and, before the end of his allotted time, he ranted to the extent of making quite an exhibition of himself. Before long an opinion was filed by the Court of Appeals reversing the judgment of the District Court, much to our gratification (86 F. 2d, 625).[63]

However, Maytag, through its counsel who was as persistent as he was disagreeable, would not give up the fight. Maytag filed a new suit out in Missouri against the General Electric Company, and the defense of the suit was assigned to another firm of patent lawyers here in New York. We offered to help them and did help them to some considerable extent, but they seemed to think they were quite equal to the task of handling the situation adequately, in fact better than we. They did their best, I am sure, but they got a licking. Then a high official of G.E., who was a friend of Mr. Davis, told him about the case and asked him if he could get a reversal. Davis's answer to that was he was confident he could get a reversal either in the Court of Appeals for the Seventh Circuit, or, if not there, then in the Supreme Court which would take the case on <u>certiorari</u> by reason of conflicting decisions of Courts of Appeals. On that confident reply, the appeal in the G.E. case was turned over to us and Mr. Davis briefed the case and argued it. He did not secure a reversal (100 F. 2d, 218)[64] but the affirmance created the conflict which enabled us to get <u>certiorari</u> granted. In the Supreme Court, Davis presented a fine argument whereas Lane encountered much difficulty and the result was a decision of the Supreme Court against the plaintiff (307 U.S. 243).[65]

This was another instance of a prolonged litigation involving two suits stemming from an unsound decision of the trial court in the first case and then going to the United States Supreme Court.

## United States Supreme Court

We have had quite a number of other cases which have gone to the Supreme Court, including George Middleton's "Dred Scott"[66] case and at least three others in which I was the advocate on one side, but the ones I have mentioned are the ones that stand out as the important ones in my recollection.

# Rainbow Light

There was another prolonged litigation, including a number of suits, which I recall with satisfaction because we achieved a large measure of success in a difficult situation and because of what it led to in the aftermath.

Back in the twenties, the "neon light" was developed to the point where it became a salable article as an advertising sign. Two companies got into the business of making and selling and servicing them and they grew to considerable size and the rivalry between them was intense. One of them was Claude Neon Lights, operating as a licensee under patents of a noted French physicist, Georges Claude. The other was known as Rainbow Light and it was dominated by a spectacular individual by the name of C.V. Bob who had had a hectic career in mining, pugilism, and various other fields. Bob had many wonderful attributes but there was a serious lack of others, notably an acceptable moral code.

The rivalry between the two companies led to a suit by Claude against a customer of Rainbow for infringement of two of the Claude patents. There was quite a trial over in Brooklyn in which Rainbow was represented by Sam Darby and ultimately there was a decision in favor of Rainbow. (31 F. 2d. 988)[67] An appeal was taken by the Claude interests, with everybody on the Rainbow side thinking of the appeal as little more than a formality because affirmance was so assured. But what happened was that the Court of Appeals reversed as to the main patent in suit, sustained the patent as valid, gave it a high place as representing a major achievement, and held that defendant infringed. (47 F. 2d. 345)[68]

The Rainbow group was completely dumbfounded. For some two or three weeks, no one in the group could evolve an idea. At that point, the President of the company showed the first sign of returning consciousness and when he intimated that he had an idea, everyone stopped where he was and awaited elucidation. Finally the President told them his idea was that they should consult other patent counsel. Pursuant to his achievement of that stupendous idea, he happened to talk with a good friend of mine for whom I had been taking out patents on link-mesh for twenty years and this friend told him he had better come around to see me. The result was that the company officials came into our office and soon they left there the enormous record of the Brooklyn suit, and, in effect, left all of their troubles there with it.

The technical development involved in the neon tube of that day was rather abstruse and before I thought I had acquired a sufficient knowledge of that technique and of all that was covered by the Brooklyn record, another suit on the Claude patent out in Los Angeles against a supplier of Rainbow tubes came on for trial. The Rainbow people asked me to attend the trial as an aid to acquiring a comprehensive knowledge of the situation, but they said I would not have to participate in the trial because they had an eminent counsel in San Francisco who would have full charge of their affairs and would manage them with great skill. Out I went to Los Angeles and another man who went out there was Raymond R. Machlett, a young man not many years out of college who had progressed to the point of being the chief technician for Rainbow. I had met him before going west but did not know him well.

The Los Angeles case came on for trial with me in attendance as a spectator. The prima facie proofs were short and soon the eminent San Franciscan had Ray Machlett on the witness stand for defendant. After an examination of a couple of hours which seemed to be nothing more than clearing away the under-brush with definitions and just when I thought he was going to deliver some telling blows, he announced that the direct examination was closed. That was at the end of the day and the court adjourned. Ray Machlett and I walked outside and looked at each other in amazement. He had not been asked to give any testimony of any moment and there was no one else who was technically informed and therefore could give some testimony of value. We had to recognize that our case was hopeless unless we two stepped in and did something about it. From then on until midnight, Ray Machlett and I were closeted together and between us we worked out a program which we thought would have some hope.

At the opening the next day, we had quite a battle over whether there could be further direct examination of the same witness by a different counsel, but we got by that and Ray and I proceeded to put in the best expert deposition we could. As a matter of fact, we did very well indeed and all the credit for it is due to Ray Machlett. He had been thinking about the case throughout the progress of the litigation up to that time and had worked out his ideas very sanely and he developed his thought on the witness stand admirably. On the whole, he conducted himself on the stand as though he had devoted his life to expert testimony. From that point on, I had to take over the conduct of the defense proofs because, while I thought my knowledge of the technical matters involved was deficient, it was quite evident that it extended way beyond any point that the San Francisco eminent had ever reached. The trial lasted for a month and there were some further proceedings in the suit extending over many months followed by a settlement which made that Los Angeles suit of no significance in the Rainbow program.

At some time during this long trial, my wife and Ray Machlett's wife arrived out there on the coast and we four returned to New York together, stopping over one day at the Grand Canyon. By the end of the trial, we had developed a bond of friendship which went on year after year and got closer and closer throughout the years up to the time when Raymond Machlett died in 1955 and Mrs. Edmonds became incapacitated, and this same close friendship extends up to the present date so far as concerns myself and Mrs. Machlett for whom I am one of two trustees for all her worldly goods.

Not long after my return to New York, activities in this neon situation sprang to fever heat, accentuated by the hatred existing between Mr. Hollingsworth who headed the Claude Neon situation and C.V. Bob who headed Rainbow, plus the resourcefulness of these two individuals in their numerous attacks and counterattacks.

The Rainbow neon tube charged to constitute infringement in the New York suit was of the type with which Rainbow started commercial business, and, within a relatively short time, it changed to a somewhat different construction, and so, when Rainbow was enjoined in the suit, it continued with the exploitation of this second type on the theory that it did not infringe; certainly it had not been held to infringe and therefore was not clearly within the injunction which had been issued. The Claude forces were outraged at this procedure which they castigated as a flouting of the judicial process and their ire rose to such a point that they initiated contempt proceedings. They applied to the Court of Appeals to administer punishment to Rainbow for contempt, and, feeling that sentencing Rainbow for contempt was not enough, they went a step further by asking the Court of Appeals to hold me personally in contempt because I had advised Rainbow it could continue with its sales notwithstanding the injunction. It was a stupid proceeding, but much else that Claude Neon did in those days under the guidance of its patent counsel was ill-advised. The presiding Judge of the Court of Appeals looked at the papers when our motion was called and then looked down at my adversary and said, "Well, what's the contempt." The adversary might just as well have gone home at that point for all the chance he had of getting anywhere.

The Court of Appeals made short shrift of the motion for contempt and sent the case back to the District Court for decision as to whether Rainbow's second construction was within the scope of the sustained patent. That led to some exceedingly interesting experiences in the District Court and later in the Court of Appeals, proceedings wherein the so-called "doctrine of equivalents" was examined at length.[69] The matter was so critical with Rainbow that I got Davis to come into it with me. We participated in the argument in both courts. Paralleling all this were other suits by Claude against Rainbow and by Rainbow against Claude, the volume being so great that Davis and I had to divide it up between us. We did not succeed in a suit against Claude but we did succeed in Claude's suits against Rainbow, and, what is most important, we secured a final ruling that the second form of the Rainbow tube was not within the protection of the Claude patent.

The Claude and Rainbow companies missed a golden opportunity to make themselves wealthy. The market for neon tubes was large and steadily growing, and, between them, they could have corralled the whole business. All they had to do was to stop fighting each other and join forces against the rest of the world. As it was, the efforts of each against the other reduced their patent assets to practically zero, with the result that anybody could go into the business and many of them did and the resulting competition took all the profit out of the business.

As the diminishing profits of Rainbow gravitated down toward the zero point, opportunities for the spectacular seemed to C.V. Bob to be diminishing too, or else he was nearing exhaustion of his capacity for scheming up new ones. So Bob decided that he might as well exit from the New York scene, and, if that was to be done, it had to be done in the grand manner — it had to be colorful and up to or beyond the Bob tradition. Having achieved this thought, action followed promptly, as it always did with C.V. Bob.

Bob had a collection of certificates of stock of Phantom Oil Company, a company which was most appropriately named because its assets were ephemeral and so was its location except as it may have been said to have a location within Bob's safe along with other certificates of the same zero value. Bob extracted some of the Phantom Oil securities from the seclusion of his safe, and had Phantom swap with Rainbow for stock of General Motors, General Electric, etc., then owned by Rainbow, Bob himself being the sole agent for both of the parties to this deal. Then he sold the securities he obtained in the trade, and then, having pocketed the cash proceeds of the sale, he departed from the scene, leaving no clue to his whereabouts. The whole country was scoured for him under warrants for his arrest for a considerable array of high crimes and misdemeanors. Bob must have gloated with satisfaction at the publicity he received. Then, after the lapse of a month or two, when the publicity had subsided to a low point, Bob stirred it all up again in characteristic fashion by walking into the office of a District Attorney in an Arizona city, with a bland, disarming smile upon his florid face, and saying, "I am told you have been looking for me." There followed arrest, various trials and final conviction and Bob exited from the picture.

# Machlett Laboratories, Inc.

When Rainbow's treasury was thus depleted and its prospects were definitely headed downward, Ray Machlett decided he had to evolve some other program for supporting his little family. Ray's father had been a pioneer in X-ray tubes and Ray had been interested, and kept abreast of developments, in that art. Also, Ray's keen mind and sound judgment brought him to a perception of an opportunity for him in the X-ray field. In this country that field had been dominated for years by General Electric Company under controlling patents, with the result that development of the art had lagged here and Ray knew there had been significant development of the X-ray technique in Europe. So, with three or four of the most promising men in the Rainbow organization, Ray set himself up in business in Long Island City making anything he could sell to users of X-ray apparatus, particularly what was known as "valve tubes". He got along for a year or two with this, developing greater stability as he went along and making a little more than enough money to live on.

Then at some time along in the summer of 1933 he telephoned me and said he would like to come up to my house in

Fairfield, Connecticut, some evening. Up he came and we sat out on the porch of my house while he told me at length about his X-ray enterprise. The gist of it was that he had made a place for himself in the X-ray business and that his enterprise would grow, but if it grew only to the extent made possible from the profits over and above what he had to use for living expenses, it would grow very slowly; and that if he could get some capital from an outside source, it would grow more rapidly. His capital needs at the moment were not great and I supplied that amount and later on I supplied some more.

By the spring of 1934, the business had grown up to the limit of the small amount of space they had on the second floor of a small building in Long Island City, and when this led to discussions of obtaining larger quarters, Ray told me there was no reason why the business should be located in New York City and that it would do quite as well outside the City, even in Connecticut. Out of this came some unusual experiences in finding a location in Connecticut. The three-story part of the building we now have was offered to us for $75,000, and we ended up by buying it for $5,000 and a mortgage. That was in 1934 when we had not progressed far from the bottom of the depression and cash money was very scarce. At that time I was working so many hours a day that I had not time for spending money and therefore had an accumulation of cash from which I enabled the company to buy the property. Before long the seller was so hard pressed for cash that he began to offer the mortgage for sale at a discount and I bought it and held it for some years until the company had funds available for buying it from me at the bargain price I had paid for it.

When we bought that building, there was a tenant on the third floor and we were told that the tenant was a chemical manufacturer. That was acceptable to us because we could use only the two lower floors at that time and we were in great need of the income from the third floor.

However, the flooring of that third floor was not the best; there were cracks here and there. At times, some of the "chemicals" produced or in use on the third floor, descended upon the second floor. Some of these "chemicals" aroused suspicion which soon developed into conviction and we came to realize that our tenant on the third floor was engaged in flaunting the prohibition laws. That placed us on the spot; we thought we could not let him stay there conducting an operation with an illicit still, but, on the other hand, we could not very well get along without the monthly check for the rent. Thus we went on month after month living with this hazard, until, fortunately for us, this unwelcome tenant got out of his own accord just about the time when the growth of our business made us want to use the third floor.

Throughout all of this, the bond of friendship with Ray Machlett became closer and closer and the business grew in volume and stability. Ray and I were the Board of Directors, and, when it was inconvenient for us to meet, we held meetings of the directors over the telephone, and as time went on we bought additions to our piece of land there in Springdale and made additions to our building.

Then along came World War II and with it a pressing need for production of electronic tubes of special types used in the war. We leased a big plant in Norwalk and installed there a most interesting operation; raw materials entered at one end of a long rectangular building, and finished tubes went out at the other end. In addition to this, we steadily increased the volume of our manufacture of X-ray tubes. By that time we had perfected the so-called rotating target X-ray tube and the war conditions created a great demand for it. Also, after the war in Europe became a hot war, and bombing from airplanes commenced, it was not long before the belligerents bombed out the production of X-ray tubes in Europe, and, as the General Electric Company in this country was busily engaged on other things, we at Machlett became practically the one and only source of X-ray tubes for the whole world and "Machlett" as the name of an X-ray tube became known wherever X-ray tubes were used and has continued so ever since.

The tubes made for the armed forces at Norwalk were not X-ray tubes; they were electronic tubes of types known as power-tubes. At the end of the war we decided to continue with the manufacture of power-tubes, but not at Norwalk; instead, we built a considerable addition to our Springdale plant and installed power-tube manufacture there, and that part of our business has grown so that now it is of greater volume than our X-ray tube manufacture.

In England, our X-ray tubes were sold during the war through a subsidiary of General Electric Company of England. It was evident to both General Electric Company and ourselves that that condition would not continue for many years after the war; instead, the manufacture of X-ray tubes in England would surely be initiated by some one. After much exchange of ideas with our friends in General Electric Company, Ray Machlett went over to London and consummated a fine deal for a British Machlett company owned by General Electric Company and ourselves. General Electric put in most of the money and we put in the designs and technique. The venture has worked out to our great satisfaction; it has been a source of revenue for us and the whole of our association with our British friends has been pleasant and harmonious even to the fulfillment of all of our aspirations.

Through the years after the war there was steady growth and broadening of the scope of our Machlett company under the masterly leadership of Ray Machlett and he built up a strong organization under him.

Our good friend, Dr. John G. Trump, a Professor on the faculty of M.I.T., was added to our Board of Directors, making a board of three which operated informally and harmoniously, and, I think, as effectively as the predecessor board of two. The business grew in volume and diversification and the plant grew in size, and, we think, the overall organization grew in skill, developing a technique in electronic tube manufacture equaled in but few other plants in the country.

The prospect for continuing growth in size and leadership developed year after year up to a time in 1953 when we were forced to recognize certain ominous portents in connection with Ray Machlett's health. As this became more and more threatening, we sent him to Memorial Hospital for a week during which he was subjected to elaborate tests and his condition was studied by a number of leaders in the study of cancer. There was no escape from the conclusion that a cancer condition had developed in one of Ray's lungs. A major operation upon the lung was considered and rejected on the conviction that Ray would not survive it. After the most careful thought and consideration by the best talent, Ray went down to M.I.T. and was given the high voltage X-ray treatment. At the end of two or three months of this treatment, we had some reason for thinking that a definite cure had been effected and he came back to his home in New Canaan and resumed his leadership in the company. Each week specimens were sent to M.I.T. for examination and each week a favorable report came back. This continued for some months, and then one time a distinctly unfavorable development was reported. From then on the condition worsened steadily. The X-ray treatment was resorted to again, but it was too rigorous for Ray in his weakened condition. We clung to hope for quite a time, but finally we had to recognize the inevitable, and on January 7, 1955, Ray passed away.

That was a grievous loss to me personally, quite apart from the blow to the prospects of our Machlett company. My close friend of twenty-five years had gone. We had worked together and played together through all those years, with never the vestige of a rift. Along with a sterling character and sound business judgment, he was a man of wide learning, active imagination, unbounded enthusiasm and irrepressible good humor, and a devoted husband and father. We were together a great deal in non-business hours, at his home and mine, all over Long Island Sound on a sailing craft in which we were part-owners for some four years, in Europe and at many places in this country. I was with him when he was awarded a citation for achievement in the scientific world by Stevens Institute, and he was with me when I was awarded an Honorary Degree by Middlebury College. He has left a vacancy with me which has not and never will be filled.

As for the company, there was nothing to do but carry on as he would have had us carry on. But a radical change had to be made in the company. Instead of the personal organization in which everything centered around Ray Machlett, a conventional business organization had to be installed. A new leader had to be selected and a working Board of Directors had to replace the rather informal board of three which was really just Ray Machlett. And the responsibility for doing this devolved on me. I had little difficulty in formulating plans, but, before proceeding with them, I had to bring others to the same views, in some instances by making them feel they were their thoughts and plans rather than mine. Then, after some three months I went to the plant one morning, stopped all work throughout the plant, and made use of our loudspeaker system to tell the whole organization what we were doing and were going to do. We installed as our successor President W.E. Stevenson, an associate of Ray Machlett in Rainbow and our Machlett company and our Vice-President in charge of all X-ray sales; and the new Board of Directors consisted of the four top operating men of the Company, the legal counsel of the Company, Dr. John G. Trump of M.I.T. and myself and I was made Chairman of the Board.

While Ray was still with us, we developed a rather ambitious program of expansion for the Company. That program we went forward with aggressively. It required the provision of more manufacturing space and more equipment and that required more capital and we accomplished the latter by selling about one and a quarter millions of dollars worth of our stock to American Research & Development Company and its associates in Boston and the Donner Trust in Philadelphia. That expansion program has gone forward steadily and favorably, so much so that for the past couple of years our sales have run over ten millions of dollars per year and we look forward to further increases, and, what is more important, the high position the Company has had in the general field of electronic tube manufacture has been well maintained.

# Retrospect

In retrospect, the practice of patent law has served me well. It has provided all of the necessary opportunity for applying engineering and for matching wits with others in the world of business, with ample rewards, financial and otherwise, for mental and physical energy applied intelligently. In addition to that, the law practice has given me close friendships with men who have meant much to me; included in them are Mr. Pennie, Fred Matthaei and Ray Machlett, as I have recorded here, and William H. Davis, whom I have mentioned many times. Other close friends and business associates of many years and now gone are Reid L. Carr and Harry A. Wilson, but those two I came to know socially before we became associated in business affairs.

Reid Carr was a gentleman and a scholar and his memory for all of the worthwhile literature he had read was prodigious, extending from Chaucer, throughout Shakespeare and down to Kipling or later, as I and many others of his host of friends knew and had occasion to marvel at time and again. He was a lawyer, a partner in the well-known firm of Clark, Carr &

## Retrospect

Ellis. He was counsel for Binney & Smith and Columbian Carbon Company for years, and, when Columbian had to install a new President back in the thirties, it succeeded in inducing him to give up professional work and assume the leadership of the Company. He was a wonderful President in all respects except that he taxed himself too severely in his presidential office with the result that he died many years before he should have, mourned by a wide circle of friends who held him in high esteem far beyond what is accorded to most humans.

Harry A. Wilson organized The H.A. Wilson Company back in World War I days and built it up very successfully. He got me to take over its patent affairs back in the twenties. Then he organized The Wilcolator Company and I participated with him in its organization and have been a director and stockholder ever since. Also, our firm has been its patent counsel from its birth to the present day. It has prospered well through the years and we have been able to make its patents very remunerative. Harry Wilson and I were close personal friends as well as business associates through all the years up to his death in 1957.

As for William H. Davis, my association with him was a very close one for over thirty years and then almost nonexistent for the past twelve years, and the abrupt change which occurred at the end of 1945 has been for me a matter of deep and continuing regret. Davis and I tried many a patent suit together, beginning with that Grand Rapids Veneer Works case to which I have referred; for many years he and I ran the affairs of the firm together, as Mr. Pennie and Marvin preferred to leave them to us; we were together in the evenings a great deal at his house and at mine; and for some years we both lived in the summers in the Fairfield, Connecticut, area. Once in a while we disagreed on how a suit should be tried or where the firm should be located or who should be the partners in the firm or something of that general nature, but always we came together on an acceptable program.

Then when World War II came along, Davis went down to Washington as Chairman of the War Labor Board, an office of an eminence which was very gratifying to him. Many leaders in the industrial world had to come before him and most of them were very deferential to him, as one would expect, and Davis got a great glow of satisfaction out of that without realizing its true nature. During Davis's absence from 1942 to September, 1945, I attempted to look after his interests in the firm, and, in my own estimation, I was never lacking in loyalty to him or proper regard for his material interests, and that was not free from difficulties because Davis, somewhat carried away by his position of prominence in the Washington scene, was impatient at times and inclined to be hasty in his comment. Even so, I think Davis got around to questioning my loyalty to him, as he did that of some others of his then partners. That has been a great regret to me in the years since Davis left the firm, the more so because there is nothing I did or neglected to do for which I have reproached myself.

Then the inevitable occurred. Davis was an idealist living down there in Washington among politicians and holders of high political office, a condition which is exceedingly apt to lead to a debacle in which the idealist is the victim. The buildup for the debacle was that Davis relinquished the office of Chairman of the War Labor Board and was rewarded for his service by being elevated to President Roosevelt's cabinet with the title of Economic Stabilizer. Roosevelt died and Davis carried on in President Truman's cabinet. Then, in September of 1945, Davis, led by his idealism, made a speech about labor rates and prices which aroused too much turmoil in the press for the politicians and that led them, Truman included, to sum-

# Retrospect

mary action which took the form of transferring all of Davis's functions to others. Davis protested and got nowhere; and, in a matter of days, he was out of office, out of Washington, and back with us.

He was with us in the New York firm for the last three months of 1945, and, on many occasions through those months, I tried to prevail upon him to come back into the firm and devote himself to the role for which he was best suited, that of a patent attorney. But Davis felt that our activities did not give him either sufficient scope or a sufficiently large audience, and also he thought that because of his conspicuous service as Chairman of the War Labor Board, the leaders of industry throughout the country would solicit his services in matters of great import to them, particularly matters concerned with labor relations. He had little realization of the extent to which he, in his administration of the War Labor Board, had incurred the hostility of leaders of industry throughout the country, their very bitter hostility. So he left us on January 1, 1946, and embarked upon the practice of law on his own. How well he has done I do not know, but I am sure he would have done better for himself had he come back with us, better financially and better for his self-esteem and better for the attainment of a high place in the field he had chosen for his major effort in the business world, that of an advocate in the field of patent law, a role for which he was blessed with talents beyond most others and far beyond any talents qualifying him in a field dominated by politicians. We have seen but little of each other in the past ten years, much to my regret.

Last, but closest of all, is my good friend James Breed. Our association began fifty years ago. We lived together as bachelors in 1910 and 1911. He was the "best man" at my wedding in Washington at the end of 1911, and before the end of 1912 I went out to Bay City, Michigan, along with quite a group of his devoted admirers under the leadership and absolute command of his brother, William C. Breed, to see to it that his marriage knot was tied effectively with appropriate proceedings both orthodox and unorthodox. Since then we have lived uptown and worked downtown near each other, and our ways in life have followed strikingly similar courses, though all the individual moves made along the way were made by each of us quite independently of the other. We started in the law practice in very humble roles and moved up from them steadily over the years with appropriate increases in the financial return for our efforts. As young married men we both took up residence on the west side of New York, and later we both moved to Park Avenue, and, still later, we both moved to Fifth Avenue. We both acquired some surplus cash before we had gone very far and both invested that surplus advantageously. And in the last moves of our respective abodes, we both used some of our surplus cash to buy apartments and we both bought in the same building. So now we are co-owners of a mutualized apartment house at 2 East 67th Street and the building is run to suit us because Jim Breed is President and I am Secretary of the tenant-owned company. In addition to all that, we have both eased off considerably in professional work in our later years and have increased correspondingly our executive work in companies we are identified with and each of us has become Chairman of the Board of Directors of the company which is his primary business interest.

The wife Jim Breed acquired back in 1912 died and in 1944 he was married to a Dear Lady who quickly won my admiration just as she had his, an admiration which has continued and deepened steadily ever since. No one is more welcome than those two at my apartment in New York or at my house at

Fairfield, and I am a frequent guest at their apartment and at their most attractive and hospitable home in Easthampton, Long Island. We play bridge together and we enjoy a libation together and our discussions cover the widest range with never a reservation on either side. Fate was kind to me when she caused the paths of the lives of Jim Breed and myself to come together. In that, as in many other ways, I have been greatly favored.

Along with all the others, I have been favored with reasonably good health — a multiplicity of minor ailments and minor deficiencies but nothing serious. So now, as I am approaching the octogenarian, I am as active as ever, and want nothing so much as to stick around for some more years to witness further development of the rivalry between autocracy and democracy, to note the progress of Pennie Edmonds in the professional field and Machlett Laboratories in the industrial field, and, more than all else, to have some participation in the progress of my son, now embarking on the career of a physicist after receiving a Ph.D. at M.I.T., and of my three grandchildren who are most promising specimens and seem to think well of their paternal grandfather. The third one of these three grandchildren is a girl and I have contrived to have her named "Penelope", with the result that she is now, and will long be, known as "Pennie Edmonds".

# Epilogue

By the 1960s, age and the nation's changing mores began to overtake Dean Edmonds. The legal profession had started losing its sense of collegiality and manners, qualities that seemingly were encoded in Dean Edmonds's DNA. Fortunately, his memoir allows us to appreciate his work in the medium in which he chose to express himself. That it forms a slim volume doesn't matter. Dean Edmonds brings to it all the size we need.

Dean Edmonds passed away on September 18, 1972 at the age of 92, while still an active member of his law firm. His lifetime and the ensuing quarter century have witnessed remarkable innovations that probably have changed the way we live and think in more ways than in the preceding two thousand years. In 1897, when Dean Edmonds embarked upon his career, the country was still in its adolescence, about to emerge from the shadows of the great powers of Europe while trying to heal the societal wounds of the Civil War. The Brooklyn Bridge and the Statue of Liberty had only recently come to grace New York's harbor, and incandescent lighting, the telephone, and the automobile were yet to come into general use. In the hundred years since, the nation endured worldwide economic calamities, outinvented, outproduced and conquered history's most powerful military regimes, and outlasted Communism's political idealogy. The airplane, radio and television, and nuclear energy emerged and ushered us into new eras of wonderment and challenge. Today, advanced telecommunications, the internet, consumer electronics, computers, plastics, pharmaceuticals, organ implants, space travel, and even the synthesis of new life forms through genetic engineering are taken more or less for granted. To the young Dean Edmonds, however, the familiar accompaniments of our contemporary life would have seemed impossible marvels.

Through it all, the institution that came to be synonymous with the name of Dean Edmonds has grown through the vitality, skill, and enterprise of the dedicated men and women of foresight who came after him. Today, it continues to bear the name of a man whose long and productive life of ninety-two years bridged the early and the contemporary years of the firm. At the end of the twentieth century, and the dawn of the next millenium, Pennie & Edmonds LLP remains as one of the largest law firms in the world specializing — as it always has — in the securing, enforcement, and commercial realization of intellectual property rights.

PENNIE & EDMONDS LLP

# ENDNOTES

## INTRODUCTION

**1.** (Page 1) Ralph Waldo Emerson, *Essays: First Series* [1841]. *Self-Reliance*.

**2.** (Page 3) Howard Edmonds, a big man known in the family as "Uncle Herc" (for Hercules). He went to Chicago on the occasion of the 1898 World's Fair there and stayed on to become a prominent banker.

## THE FIRM IN 1914

**3.** (Page 7) No trace of the floor plan of the 35 Nassau Street office exists. The earliest known address of the firm in New York City was at 5 Nassau Street, near Wall Street, during the brief period of 1910-1911.

**4.** (Page 9) According to editions of Hubbell's Legal Directory for the relevant period, Mr. Pennie formed a partnership with Mr. Goldsborough in 1890.

ENDNOTES

**5.** (Page 10) Charles J. O'Neill remained with the firm's offices in Washington, D.C. from 1908 until about 1919. During that time the Washington, D.C. branch of the firm retained the name "Pennie, Davis & Goldsborough" while the New York branch changed its name several times without Mr. O'Neill's name on it. Mr. O'Neill became a sole practitioner from 1920 to about 1923 and from 1923 to about 1930 he practiced with Alexander M. Bunn.

**6.** (Page 10) John A. Goldsborough remained with the firm in New York until 1915.

## MY ENTRANCE INTO THE PENNIE DAVIS ORGANIZATION

**7.** (Page 18) Clarence Williams Sessions (1859-1931) attended the University of Michigan and was admitted to the Michigan bar in 1883. In 1906 he became a state circuit judge, and in 1911 President Taft named him to the federal district court.

## SOME EVENTS IN THE YEARS FOLLOWING 1914

**8.** (Page 20) Frank E. Barrows worked at the firm from 1915 to 1962.

**9.** (Page 21) W. Brown Morton worked at the firm from 1915 to 1968.

**10.** (Page 21) Merton W. Sage worked at the firm from 1917 to 1958.

## THE BERLIN MILLS CASE

**11.** (Page 28) *Procter & Gamble Co. v. Berlin Mills Co.*, 256 F. 23 (2d Cir. 1919).

**12.** (Page 29) *Berlin Mills Co. v. Procter & Gamble Co.*, 254 U.S. 156, 41 S.Ct. 75, 65 L.Ed. 196 (1920).

## WIRELESS TELEGRAPHY

**13.** (Page 31) Willis H. Taylor, Jr., worked at the firm from 1919 until his death in 1982.

**14.** (Page 36) *Kintner v. Atlantic Communication Co.*, 51 F.2d 109 (S.D.N.Y. 1921).

**15.** (Page 37) *International Radio Telegraph Co. v. Atlantic Communication Co.*, 290 F. 698 (2d Cir. 1923).

## THE BESSEMERIZATION OF COPPER

**16.** (Page 41) *Pierce-Smith Converter Co. v. United Verde Copper Co.*, 293 F. 108 (D. Del. 1923).

**17.** (Page 41) *Pierce-Smith Converter Co. v. United Verde Copper Co.*, 298 F. 763 (D. Del. 1924).

**18.** (Page 41) *United Verde Copper Co. v. Pierce-Smith Converter Co.*, 7 F.2d. 13 (3d Cir. 1925).

## Endnotes

## AIR REDUCTION COMPANY

**19.** (Page 44) Airco continues today as Air Products & Chemical Co.

## THE FULLER COMPANIES

**20.** (Page 48) Nothing is known about Mr. Pennie's professional involvement with Dr. Richards.

**21.** (Page 49) The Hanna Company of Cleveland was a major factor in the American coal industry prior to World War II.

**22.** (Page 50) The so-called "Kinyon pump" was famous in its day as a device for handling coal slurries.

## RADIUM LUMINOUS PAINT

**23.** (Page 51) Little is known today of Didisheim & Company.

**24.** (Page 52) *American Radium Co. v. Hipp. Didisheim Co.*, 279 F. 601 (S.D.N.Y. 1921).

**25.** (Page 52) *American Radium Co. v. Hipp. Didisheim Co.*, 279 F. 1016 (2d Cir. 1922).

**26.** (Page 53) United States Radium Corporation was acquired in 1981 by Mitsubishi Chemical Corporation and renamed Kasei Optonix Ltd.

**27.** (Page 53) Arthur Roeder and his wife were frequent visitors to the Edmonds's home, and a close friendship developed between the two families. They were not only popular with myself and my wife, but also with my young son, who, I later discovered, developed quite a crush on Mrs. Roeder.

## OXYACETYLENE WELDING AND AMERICAN METAL PRODUCTS COMPANY

**28.** (Page 56) *Elyria Iron & Steel Co. v. American Welding & Mfg. Co.*, 15 F.2d 106 (N.D. Oh. 1923).

**29.** (Page 56) *Elyria Iron & Steel Co. v. American Welding & Mfg. Co.*, 15 F.2d 111 (6th Cir. 1926).

**30.** (Page 56) According to Dean Edmonds, Jr., Frederick Matthaei was a consummate salesman, as one had to be to do business successfully with the auto industry, for whom Matthaei's company made parts, notably the so-called torque tube that went into every Ford car prior to 1949. Matthaei got contracts by doing his homework, like knowing not to give cigars to purchasing agents that didn't smoke. He had a beautiful wife, Mildred, whom he treated with the Prussian male chauvinism that was his nature, and two sons, Frederick, Jr. and Conrad. The former attempted to take over the company after his father's death and tried to discredit Dean Edmonds by listing him as "a New York lawyer, now 80 years old," to which Mr. Edmonds responded by selling AMP to Lear-Siegler. Conrad, a Yale Whiffenpoof with a penchant and a certain amount of talent for the stage, was therefore disinherited by his father despite Dean Edmonds's advice to the contrary but endeared himself to Dean's son, whose wife was herself an opera director. Conrad eventually entered upon a stage career.

ENDNOTES

## ENLARGING CLIENTELE

**31.** (Page 60) Fibre Conduit Company eventually became the Orangeburg Marketing Corp. (see p. 54).

**32.** (Page 61) *Fiber Conduit Co. v. Bankameric Corp.*, 21 F.2d 756 (S.D.N.Y. 1927).

**33.** (Page 61) *Fiber Conduit Co. v. Bankameric Corp.*, 27 F.2d 708 (2d Cir. 1928).

## DRY KILNS FOR TREATING LUMBER

**34.** (Page 68) *Henderson v. Welch Dry Kiln Co.*, 26 F.2d 810 (E.D. La. 1928).

**35.** (Page 68) *Henderson v. Welch Dry Kiln Co.*, 39 F.2d 589 (5th Cir. 1930)

**36.** (Page 71) *Gilchrist-Fordney Co. v. Welch Dry Kiln Co.*, 33 F.2d 117 (5th Cir. 1929).

## RUBBER ACCELERATORS

**37.** (Page 72) Allied Chemical later became Allied-Signal, Inc., an aerospace company. Most recently, Allied-Signal merged with Honeywell, Inc. to become Honeywell International, Inc.

**38.** (Page 73) *Dovan Chemical Corp. v. National Aniline & Chemical Co.*, 292 F. 555 (2d Cir. 1923).

**39.** (Page 73) *Dovan Chemical Corp. v. Corona Cord Tire Co.*, 10 F.2d 598 (W.D. Pa. 1926).

**40.** (Page 74) *Dovan Chemical Co. v. Corona Cord Tire Co.*, 16 F.2d 419 (1926, rehearing denied, 1927).

**41.** (Page 74) *Corona Cord Tire Co. v. Dovan Chemical Corp.*, 276 U.S. 358, 48 S.Ct. 380, 72 L.Ed. 610 (1928).

**42.** (Page 75) *Hayes v. Surface Combustion Corp.*, 18 F.Supp. 871 (S.D.N.Y. 1937).

**43.** (Page 75) *Hayes v. Surface Combustion Corp.*, 96 F.2d. 61 (2d Cir. 1938).

**PELLETTED CARBON BLACK**

**44.** (Page 80) The Columbian Carbon Company was not only a client but an organization in which Dean Edmonds reportedly took a particular interest when his good friend Reid L. Carr became president. He and his wife, a former Danish princess, came to be among the Edmonds family's best friends, so much so that the Edmonds children called them Uncle Reid and Aunt Eleanora, and Mrs. Edmonds was fascinated to have found her match in a man who could recite as much Shakespeare as she could. Note further details about Reid Carr on page 102.

**45.** (Page 81) *Binney & Smith Co. v. United Carbon Co.*, 37 F.Supp. 779 (S.D. W.Va. 1941).

**46.** (Page 81) *Binney & Smith Co. v. United Carbon Co.*, 125 F.2d. 255 (4th Cir. 1942).

ENDNOTES

**47.** (Page 82) *United Carbon Co. v. Binney & Smith Co.*, 317 U.S. 228, 63 S.Ct. 165, 87 L.Ed. 232 (1942).

**48.** (Page 82) U.S. law still requires that patent claims be "definite" in their recitation of the invention by particularly pointing out and distinctly claiming the subject matter sought to be patented. 35 U.S.C. Section 112.

**49.** (Page 82) The "Board" referred to here is known today as the Board of Patent Appeals and Interferences, the appellate tribunal within the Patent and Trademark Office.

**50.** (Page 83) Unlike applications for original patents, the filings of reissue patent applications, to correct mistakes in original patents, are published in the weekly Official Gazette of the Patent and Trademark office.

**51.** (Page 83) See 28 U.S.C. ßß 2201 and 2202 (the Declaratory Judgment Act).

**52.** (Page 83) A case is said to be "at issue" when all of the pleadings have been made.

**53.** (Page 84) *United Carbon Co. v. Carbon Black Research Foundation, Inc.*, 59 F.Supp. 384 (D. Md. 1945).

## UNITED STATES SUPREME COURT

**54.** (Page 87) The United States Court of Claims is today called the United States Claims Court and its jurisdiction remains over suits against the U.S. Government.

**55.** (Page 87) *Electric Boat Co. v. United States*, 57 Ct. Cl. 497 (Ct. Cl. 1922).

**56.** (Page 88) *Electric Boat Co. v. United States*, 263 U.S. 621, 44 S.Ct. 224, 68 L.Ed. 478 (1924).

**57.** (Page 89) The Air Reduction (Airco) suit involved a catalyst that promoted the reaction forming ethylene oxide. One of Dean Edmonds's expert witnesses in the case was a man by the name of Hugh S. Taylor, who was supposedly a chemist of some distinction. He reportedly had also had some kind of interlude with the Pope, who had bestowed on him the title of "Excellency". Under cross-examination he demanded to be addressed by that title whenever the opposing attorney spoke to him, a procedure that so unnerved that gentleman that Dr. Taylor may have materially helped to win the case. He subsequently became Dean of Princeton University Graduate School, so that Dean Edmonds was keen to have his son do his postgraduate work there. Stockett did, in fact, take a master's degree at Princeton, but missed M.I.T. so much that he returned there for his doctorate. That decision was also prompted by the fact that the grandson, Dean III, was on the way, and Stockett preferred the obstetric care in Boston to that available in Princeton.

**58.** (Page 89) *Carbide & Carbon Chemical Corp. v. U.S. Industrial Chemicals, Inc.*, 34 F.Supp. 813 (D. Md. 1940).

**59.** (Page 89) *United States Industrial Chemicals, Inc. v. Carbide & Carbon Chemicals Corp.*, 121 F.2d 665 (4th Cir. 1941).

**60.** (Page 89) *U.S. Industrial Chemicals, Inc. v. Carbide & Carbon Chemicals Corp.*, 315 U.S. 668, 62 S.Ct. 839, 86 L.Ed. 1105 (1942).

## ENDNOTES

**61.** (Page 90) *U.S. Industrial Chemicals, Inc. v. Carbide & Carbon Chemicals Corp.*, 67 F.Supp. 895, 71 U.S.P.Q. 226 (S.D.N.Y. 1946)

**62.** (Page 91) *Maytag Co. v. Brooklyn Edison Co.*, 11 F.Supp. 743 (E.D.N.Y. 1935).

**63.** (Page 92) *Maytag Co. v. Brooklyn Edison Co.*, 86 F.2d 625 (2d Cir. 1936).

**64.** (Page 92) *General Electric Supply Corp. v. Maytag Co.*, 100 F.2d 218 (8th Cir. 1938).

**65.** (Page 92) *Maytag Co. v. Hurley Machine Co.*, 307 U.S. 243, 59 S.Ct. 857, 83 L.Ed. 1264 (1939).

**66.** (Page 93) No record can be found regarding the usage of the term "Dred Scott" case in the context in which it is used here.

## RAINBOW LIGHT

**67.** (Page 95) *Claude Neon Lights, Inc. v. Rainbow Light, Inc.*, 31 F.2d 988 (S.D.N.Y. 1927).

**68.** (Page 95) *Claude Neon Lights, Inc. v. Rainbow Light, Inc.*, 47 F.2d 345 (E.D.N.Y. 1931).

**69.** (Page 98) The so-called "doctrine of equivalents", first enunciated patent cases in the mid-nineteenth century, remains viable today as a means whereby a court, in a situation where the claims of a patent are not literally infringed, can deem them to be infringed nonetheless when the differences that distinguish the claims from the offending product or process are insubstantial.

# INDEX

"A man who is his own attorney has
   a fool for a client" .................68
"Assistant Patent Attorney" ..............6
"Civil Service" .....................3
"doctrine of equivalents" ................98
"neon light"..........................94
"stitch-weld" .........................59
"the Mouse" ..........................8
"valve tubes" .........................101
"watch dogs of the Treasury" ........88
A.H. Grebe Company ......................31
Addresses
   2 East 67th Street .....................112
   17th and F Streets........................4
   35 Nassau Street...........................
   ......7, 10, 14, 22, 23, 25, 42, 44, 64
   165 Broadway ...............................
   ................22, 30, 42, 44, 50, 64, 65
   247 Park Avenue ......................65
   342 Madison Avenue ..........44-45
Air Reduction ..............................44, 89
Airco ....................44-47, 54-56
Albany ....................................9
Alien Property Custodian ..............33,
Allentown-Catasauqua region ........48
Allied Chemical ...........................72
Alternating current ..........................59
American Bar Association................62
American Merchant Marine ..............3
American Metal Products
   Company..........................57
American Patent Law
   Association ..........................62
American Research & Development
   Company..........................107

American Smelting and Refining ..39
Anaconda ..........................................39
Apartment in New York ................112
Application for reissue ....................82
Arendt, Professor Morton................30
Arizona .............................................100
Arlington Hotel ................................3
Armstrong, Edwin ................30, 32, 37
   feedback or regenerative circuit
   patents ..........................................30
Army contracts ...................................24
Artificial lard................................26, 86
Artificial limbs ..................................25
Association of the Bar of the City of
   New York ....................................62
Atlantic Communication Company
   .................................................31, 37
Auditor for the War Department......4
Autocracy and democracy, rivalry
   between .....................................113
Automobile tires........................80, 81

Babcock & Wilcox..............................50
Baekeland, George ............................65
Bakelite Company ............................65
Baltimore ..............................83, 89-90
Bankers Club......................................78
Bar Associations ................................62
Bar of the District of Columbia ........5
Bar of the State of New York ............9
Barksdale, Judge................................81
Barrows, Frank E.
   ..........20, 21, 25-28, 72, 86, 89, 90
Basic-lined copper converters ..38, 40
Bay City, Michigan .........................112

126

# INDEX

Belknap, Mr. .................................17, 18
Berlin Mills .....................25, 26, 28, 41
Betts, L.F.H. ........................................34
Betts, Sheffield & Betts
 .............................9, 11, 30, 34, 36
Binney & Smith Company
 ............................................80, 81, 109
Binney, Mr. ..........................................80
Blackman, Mr. ....................................39
Blackstone ............................................5
Board of Appeals ........................82-83
Board of Directors
 ....................53, 103, 105, 107, 112
Bob, C.V. ........................94, 97, 99, 100
Bosch Magneto Company of
 Germany ........................................7
Breed, Abbott & Morgan ..................58
Breed, James McV. ............................58
 second wife of ..........................112
 "best man" at Edmonds's
 1911 wedding ..........................111
Breed, William C. .......................58, 112
Breed, William C., Jr. ........................58
Bridge .................................................113
British Machlett company ..............104
Broad Street ........................................78
Broadway .....................................14, 22
Brooklyn Court ..................................91
Brooklyn Edison Company ............90
Brumbaugh, Granville ......................78
Brumbaugh, Free, Graves and
 Donohue .....................................79
Bull, Edgar ..........................................87
Bureau of Navigation .....................3-4
Butte, Montana ............................38, 39
Byers, Judge .......................................91

Cables to Europe ...............................32
Campbell, Worthington ....................78
Cancer, High voltage X-ray
 treatment of ............................105
Capitol Hill ..........................................4
Carbon black ...................80, 81, 85, 86
Carr, Reid L. .....................................108
Central High School ...........................2
Certiorari .....................28, 74, 82, 89, 92
Charleston, West Virginia ................81
Chase Manhattan National Bank ....13
Chicago, Illinois ..........3, 12, 38, 62, 91

Choate, Joseph ...................................86
Church Street ....................................22
Cincinnati .......................27, 56, 59, 60
City Investing Building ...................22
City Lunch Club ...............................22
City of Grand Rapids .......................16
Civil War ..............................................4
Clark, Carr & Ellis ..................108-109
Claude, Georges ................................94
Claude Neon Lights ......94, 95, 97, 98
Cleveland, Ohio ....................49, 54, 56
Cleveland, President ..........................2
Coe, Commissioner ..........................83
Coleman, Judge ...................84, 89, 90
Collyer, Mrs. .......................................8
Colorado Fuel and
 Iron Corporation .....................53
Columbia University ..................30, 32
Columbian Carbon Company
 ............................................80, 81, 85, 109
Combustion Engineering ................50
Commissioner of Navigation ........3, 4
Committees on Commerce of the
 Senate and the House .................4
Connecticut ..................66, 78, 102, 109
Copper companies ............................39
Copper matte ....................................38
Copper mining .................................38
Corona Cord Tire Company ............73
Cortlandt Street ................................22
Cottonseed oil ...................................26
Court of Appeal 28, 36, 41, 47, 52, 56,
 59-61, 71, 74-76, 81, 82, 84, 89-90,
 .................................91, 92, 95, 98
Court of Appeals for the Fourth
 Circuit .........................................81
Court of Appeals in Cincinnati
 .........................................56, 59, 60
Court of Claims ...........................87-88
Coxe, Judge .......................................90
Crisco .................................................26
Cutting and welding torches ..........47

Darby, Sam ...................................90, 95
Davis, Albert G. .................5, 10, 11, 76
Davis, Honorable John W. ..............73
Davis, William H. 1, 7, 8, 10-14, 17-21,
 23, 30, 40, 45, 48, 64, 74, 86, 87, 89,
 .................91, 92, 98, 108, 109-111

127

Chairman of the War Labor
  Board ............................................110
  Mother-in-law of .......................8
Davis-Bournonville Company ........47
Davis-Bournonville decision ..........86
De Forest, Lee ...................30, 33, 34, 36
  patent................................33, 34, 36
December 20, 1879 (birthdate) ..........2
Delaware District Court ..................39
Democrats ...............................................2
Depression.........................................102
Detroit .............................17, 18, 55, 56
Dienner, John ......................................62
Diphenylguanidine .....................72, 73
District Court at Baltimore .............83
District Court in New York
  .........................................27, 72, 75
Donner Trust in Philadelphia........107
Dorr, Goldthwaite .............................24
Dovan Chemical Company ............72
DuPont..................................................73

Easthampton, Long Island .............113
Eastman Kodak Company ................8
Economic Stabilizer ........................110
Edmonds & Edmonds ......................13
Edmonds, Dean S. .............................13
  graduation from high school ....2
  grandchildren of.......................113
  New York Patent Law
  Association, president of,
  1941-42.........................................62
Edmonds, Howard...............................3
Edmonds, Mrs. ...................................97
Edmonds, Penelope ("Pennie") ....113
Edmonds, Samuel O. ..................5, 115
Electric Boat Company ....................87
Electronic tubes ...............................103
Elyria Iron & Steel Company
  ...........................................54, 59, 60
Emery, Frederick................................87
Equitable Building ............................44
Equity Rules .......................................18
Ethylene oxide case ..........................88
Europe ....................32, 51, 101, 104, 106
Examiner .............................9, 11, 45, 82
Examiners-in-Chief ...........................83

False testimony ..................................75

Fairfield, Connecticut ......78, 102, 109
F.B.I. .....................................................76
Fessenden patents......30-31, 33, 34, 35
Fibre Conduit Company ............60, 61
Fifth Avenue ....................................112
Fish, Frederick P.........................11, 87
Fish, Richardson,
  Herrick & Storrow .....................11
Flintkote...............................................65
Foreign patent matters .......................7
Free, Walter ........................................78
French language ..................................9
Fuller, Colonel ..............................48-50
Fuller Engineering Company..........48
Fuller-Lehigh Company ..................48

General Dynamics Company ..........87
General Electric Company
  ........5, 11, 12, 31, 76, 92, 101, 104
  Patent Department of
  ........................................5, 6, 11, 12
General Motors..................................99
Georgetown University
  Law School ....................3, 5, 8, 11
German language ...............................9
German technicians .........................33
Germany ..............................7, 9, 31, 33
Gettysburg, Battle of .........................4
Gibson, Judge .............................73, 74
Gifford & Bull ....................................40
Gifford, Mr. ..................................40, 87
Goethals, General ...................23-24, 87
Goldsborough, John A. .....................9
Grand Canyon ...................................97
Grand Central area ..........................64
Grand Rapids, Michigan.................15
Grand Rapids Veneer Works ..15, 109
Grebe, A.H. ........................................31
Guaranty Trust Company ...............21
Guggenheim officialdom ................39

H.A. Wilson Company ..................109
Handwriting expert .........................73
Hand, Judge Learned ...............46, 75
Hanna Company of
  Cleveland ...................................49
Hanover Bank Building...................10
Hazeltine, Prof. .................................37
Heat-treating furnace......................75

128

# INDEX

Herrick, Farren, Chase and Pennie ..9
Hipp. Didisheim & Company ..51, 53
Hoguet & Neary ............................77, 78
   Edmonds's "fee for acting as the
   marriage broker" for .................78
Hoguet, Neary & Campbell ............78
Hoguet, Ramsay ...........................77, 78
Hollingsworth, Mr. ...........................97
Holmes, Associate Justice Oliver
   Wendell .......................................88
Holmes, District Judge E.R. ............68
Hopkins, Clarence .........................8, 14
House at Fairfield ....................112-113
Hudson River ....................................23
Hughes, Charles Evans ....................28
Hydrogenation .................................26

Interference Division ..........................9
Interference proceeding....................15
International Association for the
   Protection of Industrial Property,
   American Group of ..................62

Jealousy of "the mistress" ..........62, 63
Judge Advocate General .....................5

Katadin Iron Works ..........................10
Kilns for drying lumber ...................67
Kinyon pump ....................................50
Knoxville, Tennessee ........................10

Laboratory record book....................73
Lacombe, Honorable
   E. Henry ................................34, 36
Ladas, Dr. Stephen ...........................62
L'air Liquide .....................................44
Lane, Wallace R. ..........................12, 91
Lard substitute .................................26
Latin, knowledge of............................5
Lawrence Mfg. Co. v. Janesville ......53
Lawyers Club ....................................22
Lehigh University .............................48
Lehmann, Herbert ............................24
Liberty Street ...................7, 13, 20, 21
Liberty Tower Building ..............13, 14
Link-mesh .........................................95
London ............................................104
Long Island City .....................101, 102
Long Island Sound .........................106

Los Angeles ................................95-97

Machlett, Mrs. ...................................97
Machlett, Raymond R...............96, 101
   Honorary Degree from
   Middlebury ..............................106
Maine .........................................10, 26
Manton, Judge Martin T........72, 75, 76
Marconi, Guglielmo ........11, 30, 33-36
   patents ..................................11, 30
Marvin, Arba B.
   ............1, 7, 12, 20, 21, 45, 49, 109
Master in accounting proceeding ..34
Matthaei, Frederick C.........56, 57, 108
May, Marcus B. ............................26, 29
Mayer, Judge Julius ....................36, 52
Maytag Company ......................90, 92
McKinley, President William ............2
Memorial Hospital .........................105
Merchant, Ernest....................44-46, 54
Metallurgy .........................................10
Metzger, Dr.......................................45
Middleton, George ...........................93
   "Dred Scott" case of ................93
Military Court.....................................5
Mississippi (Biloxi)...........................68
Missouri ............................................92
M.I.T. .......................67, 105, 107, 113
Mobile, Alabama ..............................68
Morris, Judge ........................40, 82, 84
Mahoney, Daniel V. ....................64, 75
Morton, W. Brown ......................21, 64
Mutual Life Building at Nassau and
   Liberty Streets ..........................13

Nassau Street
   7, 10, 13, 21-23, 25, 42, 44, 48, 64
National Aniline & Chemical
   Company....................................72
National Electrical Products
   Company....................................61
Neary, Jack ...............................40, 77-79
Neave, Mr. ........................................56
Neutrodyne .......................................37
New Canaan ...................................105
New Hampshire ...............................26
New Jersey, partners who lived in 64
New Jersey Zinc Company..............10
New Orleans ...............................67-68

New York City .............5, 75, 102, 112
New York Harbor..............................23
New York Patent Law
   Association ..................................62
New York subways ..........................75
Norwalk, Connecticut ....................104

O'Neill, Charles J..............................10
Orangeburg Manufacturing
   Company......................................61
Original record, alteration of ..........75
Oxyacetylene torch ....................54, 59

Paper manufacturing procedure ....26
Park Avenue ...........................65, 112
Parker, Judge ..............................81-82
Parkinson & Lane.............................12
Paris ...............................................24, 40
Patent Office .......................9, 11, 12, 82
Peace Commission......................24, 40
Peirce-Smith Converter
   Company................................39, 41
Pennie & Goldsborough ..............9, 10
Pennie, Davis & Goldsborough
   .....................................7, 10, 14, 20
Pennie, Davis & Marvin ..................20
Pennie, Davis, Marvin & Edmonds
   ......................................................1, 21
Pennie, Edmonds, Morton, Barrows
   and Taylor.......................................1
Pennie, Goldsborough & O'Neill....10
Pennie, John C.
   1, 7, 9, 10, 14-18, 20, 21, 23-27,
   ......................................38-44, 46, 48, 80
Pennsylvania Avenue .....................2, 4
Phantom Oil Company .....................99
Pine and Nassau Streets .....................9
Pittsburgh, Pennsylvania ..........61, 73
Plattsburg, New York, Officers
   Training Camp at......................23
Powdered coal..............................48-50
Power-tubes ....................................104
Presidency .....................28, 53, 74
President
   2, 15, 16, 28, 46, 53, 55, 57, 59, 62,
   ........67, 76, 95, 107, 109, 110, 112
President McKinley .............................2
President Roosevelt's cabinet ........110
Primary Examiner ............................82

Proctor & Gamble Company ..........26
Prohibition laws ........................69, 103

Radio Corporation of America
   (R.C.A.) ..................................31, 37
Radium paint .............................51, 53
Rainbow Light..............94-98, 101, 107
Rainbow neon tube, the ..................97
Reinforcing agent ..............................80
Reissue patent........................83, 85, 89
Republican Club................................37
Republicans.................................2, 37
Richards, Dr. ......................................48
Rochester, New York ..........................8
Roeder, Mr. Arthur............................53
Rolling steel strip ..............................54
Rosenthal, Leon ..................................7
Rotating target X-ray tube ............103
Rubber accelerators ...............72, 80, 86
Rubber manufacturing industry ....72
Rubber plants ....................................81

Sage, Merton W. ..............21, 40, 67, 68
Sayville circuit ..................................32
Sayville, Long Island ..................31-34
Sayville Telefunken
   wireless service ........................32
Schenectady ..........................5, 9, 11-13
Sessions, Judge ..................................18
Sheffield, Mr ......................................36
Smith, Mr. ............................80, 81, 109
Smith, E.A. Cappelen ..................38-40
   U.S. Patent 943, 280 ..................39
Soap manufacture ............................26
Sound reproduction............................8
Springdale ........................................104
Steel tubing .......................................54
Stevens Institute of Technology ....106
Stevenson, W.E .................................107
Swan, Judge ......................................75
Swiss watches ..............................51, 53

Taft, Chief Justice .............................74
Taylor, Willis ................................31, 37
Telefunken....................................31, 32
The Hague, Holland ........................62
Third Pennsylvania Cavalry..............4
Thwing, Mr........................................16
Traffic Agreement.............................32

130

# INDEX

Transatlantic wireless telegraphy
    radio ........................................ 31, 32
Treasury Department .......... 3, 4, 5, 88
Truman, President Harry S ............ 110
Trump, Dr. John G .................. 105, 107
Tube-welding litigation .................... 59

Union Carbide ................................. 65
Union College .................................... 9
United Carbon Company .......... 81, 83
United States Circuit Court
    in New York ............................... 34
United States Court of Claims ........ 87
United States Radium
    Corporation ............................... 53
United States Supreme Court
    ................................ 25, 47, 86, 92
United Verde Copper Company
    ................................................ 39-41
Universities of Goettingen
    and Breslau ................................... 9
University of Michigan,
    eminent scientist from .............. 84
University of Wisconsin .................. 12
U.S. Industrial Chemicals .......... 88-89
U.S.A., as client ................................ 36

Virginia ............................................ 81
Vulcanization .................................... 72

Walker Brothers ............................... 60
Wall Street location .......................... 66
War Department ................................ 4
War Labor Board ...................... 110, 111
Washing machines ........................... 90
Washington, D.C.
    ..2-5, 8-11, 24, 25, 45, 64, 110, 111
Webster, Daniel ................................ 86
Wedding in Washington ................ 111
Welch, Mr. .................................. 67-70
Welch Dry Kiln Company ................ 67
Welding ...................... 47, 54, 59, 60, 86
    patents ..................................... 59, 60
West Virginia ................................... 81
Westchester, partners living in ........ 66
Western Union ................................. 18
Westinghouse ............................. 30, 31
Whittemore, Hulbert & Belknap .... 17
Wick, Myron .............................. 59, 60
Wilcolator Company ...................... 109

Wilmington, Delaware .............. 40, 82
Wilson, Harry A. .................... 108, 109
Winder Building ................................ 4
Wireless telegraphy .................... 30, 31
Wisconsin .................................... 12, 52
Woolsey, Judge ............................ 75, 76
Woolworth Building ........................ 27
World War I
    ........ 22, 23, 33, 37, 48, 51, 87, 109
World War II ............................ 103, 110

X-ray tubes ...................... 101, 103, 104

Years
    1858 ................................................ 9
    1877 ................................................ 9
    1879 ............................................ 2, 9
    1881 ................................................ 9
    1897 ................................................ 2
    1900 .............................................. 11
    1901 .............................................. 11
    1903 .............................................. 11
    1904 .............................................. 11
    1905 .......................................... 6, 12
    1908 .............................................. 10
    1910 ............................................ 111
    1911 ............................................ 111
    1912 ..................................... 111, 112
    1913 .............................................. 30
    1914 ........................... 7-9, 19, 20, 31
    1915 ........................... 19, 20, 25, 31
    1916 ................................. 23, 39, 44
    1917 ....................................... 21, 32
    1919 ................................... 22, 24, 39
    1920 .............................................. 42
    1921 ....................................... 41, 43
    1933 ............................................ 101
    1934 ............................................ 102
    1940 ....................................... 64, 66
    1942 ............................................ 110
    1945 ..................................... 109-111
    1946 ............................................ 111
    1947 .............................................. 62
    1953 ............................................ 105
    1955 ....................................... 97, 106
    1957 ............................................ 109

Zenith Corporation ......................... 37
Zinc oxide ........................................ 80